HUNTING MATURE WHITETAILS
THE LAKOSKY WAY

QUALITY DEER MANAGEMENT
WITH LEE & TIFFANY LAKOSKY
BY DUNCAN DOBIE

Copyright ©2011 F+W Media, Inc.

Published by

Krause Publications, a division of F+W Media, Inc.
700 East State Street • Iola, WI 54990-0001
715-445-2214 • 888-457-2873
www.krausebooks.com

To order books or other products call toll-free 1-800-258-0929
or visit us online at www.krausebooks.com or www.Shop.Collect.com

ISBN-13: 978-1-4402-2389-1
ISBN-10: 1-4402-2389-0

Cover Design by Al West
Designed by Paul Birling
Edited by Brian Lovett

Printed in United States of America

DEDICATION

First and foremost, we'd like to thank our families, who still love, understand and tolerate us even though we have been absent from all holidays, funerals, births, weddings, baptisms and birthdays during the hunting season for more than a decade. Without your continued love and support, we couldn't continue on this incredible journey that we love so much.

A special thank you to our parents, Linda and Leonard, who stood by us and believed in us, even when everyone else thought we were crazy. And to our friend, mentor and brother in Christ, David Blanton. We love you all.

Thank you to all of our sponsors, business associates and, most of all, our fans. You are the best.

Never in a million years did we think we would be living this impossible dream. Without the generosity and support of Tom Roles and John Benike, none of this would have been possible. We are forever grateful to you both. There are always tree stands with your names on them down here. We love you guys.

Finally, a sincere debt of gratitude to Duncan Dobie, who endured hours of our ramblings and hunting stories, all while sitting in the uncomfortable buddy seat of our tractor. The fact that you were able to take it all and make sense of it is truly remarkable. You're amazing.

In loving memory of Joan Lakosky and Gary Profant.

— Lee and Tiffany

ABOUT THE AUTHOR

Duncan Dobie has been a full-time outdoor writer for more than 30 years. The author of more than 1,500 articles, his stories and photographs have appeared in numerous books, magazines and newspapers across the country. Most of his articles are about white-tailed deer and whitetail hunting. He was a regular contributor to *North American Whitetail* magazine for more than 25 years. He is the author of six previous books, four of which are about white-tailed deer.

Duncan became editor of *North American Whitetail* magazine in 2004, a position he held until late 2009, at which time he returned to free-lancing. Duncan lives in Marietta, Ga., with his wife, Kappi, of more than 40 years. They have two daughters and five grandchildren.

QR CODES

Scan this QR code with your smartphone to view bonus video footage of big deer mentioned in this book.

HUNTING MATURE WHITETAILS
THE LAKOSKY WAY

CONTENTS

LEE AND TIFFANY: THAT SPECIAL MAGIC

Like many other avid whitetail hunters across the country, I've followed the meteoric rise to fame of America's best-known hunting couple for several years. Six or seven years ago, I first saw them on their popular TV show *Gettin' Close*, and I noticed right away there was something about this husband-and-wife team — something special that's hard to put your finger on.

I wasn't the only one who noticed this phenomenon. Tens of thousands of other hunters like me also saw it. What we saw was a combination of personality, charisma, intelligence, charm, camera presence and a special connection to us, the deer hunters of America, that made us welcome this all-American couple, Lee and Tiffany, into our living rooms every week as if they were old friends.

Tiffany — with her beautiful blond hair, big brown eyes and a smile that could melt an iceberg, along with her bubbly, spontaneous personality and adventurous spirit — quickly won the hearts of thousands of whitetail hunters of all ages and from all walks of life. She truly was — and is — the girl next door.

G.B.   S.C.g.   A.t.Rb.

K.B·C.B.   K.M.

P.W.

To say that Lee and Tiffany are the most famous deer hunting couple in America today would be an understatement. But fame is a fleeting thing, and the fame they have attained was never intentional. The special magic that defines Lee and Tiffany is not anything you can manufacture or create. It simply happens.

When they're not making personal appearances or doing countless farm and management chores, Lee and Tiffany spend many hours filming their top-rated TV show, *The Crush*.

As such, she also won the hearts of wives, mothers and grandmothers who might have been joining their husbands afield. If they weren't actually doing it, they were certainly thinking about it, and chances are they even tried it after watching Tiffany, because she makes it look so easy. Then there were the children — especially the sons and daughters of hunters, but particularly the daughters, who want to be just like Tiffany — who idolize her and look up to her as an icon.

Lee also brought his own special blend of talents to the table. Smart, handsome and never afraid of working long hours to achieve his goals, this young man also had great camera presence. (Some might correctly guess that he's obsessed with whitetail hunting, but when you love what you do as much as he does, it's easy to be passionate about every facet of your life.)

Putting all the TV and celebrity hype aside, Lee is a gifted hunter who has been studying whitetails for most of his adult life, and he is a virtual encyclopedia of knowledge when it comes to hunting big, mature bucks.

I dare say there might only be a handful of other hunters in North America who can match his storehouse of knowledge or experience. More important, however, he is an amazing and dedicated bow-hunter. Early in his TV adventures, he quickly showed us in a no-nonsense way that with a good knowledge of the subject, a lot of self-restraint, and determination and hard work, it's possible for any serious hunter to shoot an outstanding whitetail — maybe even the buck of a lifetime.

To say that Lee and Tiffany are the most famous deer hunting couple in America today would be an understatement. But fame is a fleeting thing, and the fame they have attained was never intentional. Lee, although

a single-minded individual, never set his sights on having his own TV show. He simply had a passion for hunting big bucks, and he pursued that passion with an almost super-human energy for so many years that it eventually opened doors and paved the way for the amazing success that followed.

It was never planned. It just happened, like an ocean tsunami that could not be stopped, and now the couple's fame has reached epic proportions. And they'll tell you the same thing again and again: "We just loved the hunting life, and we started doing it because we loved it so much, and we loved doing it together."

The special magic that defines Lee and Tiffany is not anything you can manufacture or create. It simply happens. When it manifests itself in the form of a hunting couple like Lee and Tiffany, people notice it right away, and it takes on a life of its own. In

a brief time, this Iowa couple has grown to be America's most beloved husband-and-wife hunting team. Certainly, they have attained the American dream, and like so many successful people before them, they make it look ridiculously easy.

But "easy" is not a word in this hard-working couple's vocabulary. To be blunt, when they're not out making appearances or hunting somewhere during the season, they work extremely long hours doing countless farm and management chores whenever they are at home during the off-season. When hunting season opens in late summer (they usually go elk and mule deer hunting in early September), they hunt almost every day like there's no tomorrow.

During planting season, which often includes most of April, May, June, July and August, Lee is frequently on a tractor from daylight to well beyond dark. When he gets home at night, do you think he sits down to rest and watch TV? Most people would be exhausted after having put in 10 to 12 hours on a tractor, but instead of relaxing, he and Tiffany are usually up well into the early-morning hours catching up on paper work and correspondence, or doing a thousand other tasks required of them. At various times of year, Lee also spends many hours at night poring over the thousands of trail camera photos he gets each month.

Lee and Tiffany are night owls who are constantly juggling a dozen tasks at once. For years, they've operated on only a few hours of sleep. Then, they're up early and raring to go the next morning, ready to do it again. Their energy is boundless. They don't go on vacations in the normal sense. Every day is a vacation to them, especially when they are working together on the farm. They truly love going out and making appearances at deer shows and other events, and they live for hunting season. But being together on the farm and spending an evening together at home is something they truly cherish.

If you take your average definition of passion and determination and multiply it by, say, 50, you might begin to have an idea of who Lee really is. And Tiffany is right up there beside him. While Lee is on the tractor disking or planting, Tiffany and her mom, Linda, might be taking their trusty old Ford truck — with 220,000 miles on it — into town to buy more seed or fertilizer. Or they might be out moving equipment from one farm to another, supporting Lee in every way.

No, being Lee and Tiffany is not the Hollywood life of leisure that TV might lead us to believe. But for this hard-working couple, it's the life they have chosen because they love it so much. Everything they do is a labor of love, and it shows because they do it so well. Lee and Tiffany complement each other in so many ways.

The thought, time and energy Lee puts into managing and hunting the farms he and Tiffany hunt are extraordinary. There is no extreme he will not explore and no technique that he won't use if he thinks it will benefit his goal of being able to grow, protect and target mature 5- to 6-year-old bucks.

Lee is also a very enterprising individual. How many people do you know who love to hunt so much that they finagled a way to skip school in college so they could hunt almost every day and take off nearly the entire month of November? That would be Lee. And he still breezed through college with fantastic grades.

15

How many college graduates have you heard of who get a job working shifts so they could continue hunting almost every day during deer season and take off almost all of November — just like in his college days — without getting fired? Not many. Only Lee could have pulled off those feats. Why did he do it? Hunting has always been the most important thing in his life, with the exception of Tiffany. Now, because they are a team, hunting is the most important thing in both of their lives.

Lots of young men who love to hunt dream about getting a job that will let them live their dream and make a living in the hunting industry. But in reality, very few ever achieve that dream. Lee never really wasted much time dreaming about how

he could get where he wanted to go. To him, deer hunting was so all-consuming that he simply did it day in and day out, come what might. Then after he met Tiffany, they did it together.

The Lakosky hit list of bucks Lee and Tiffany plan to target each year is almost legendary. Of course, Lee's management program has been incredibly successful, and the couple has so many great places to hunt in Iowa and Kansas. Therefore, several of the bucks on the annual hit list make it through the season unscathed by default. But that's OK, because Lee knows those bucks will only be bigger and better when the next season rolls around.

In August 2011, while working on this book, I had the pleasure of spending some time with Lee and Tiffany while they were on the road making appearances at several Bass Pro Shops stores in Indiana, Tennessee and North Carolina. Whenever Lee and Tiffany make appearances at deer shows or outdoor stores, they generate long lines of dedicated fans who come to see them. And

often, those fans stand in line for hours just to shake the hands of Lee and Tiffany, or maybe get an autograph or picture.

At the Indiana store, the four-hour event ended at 9 p.m. At that time, however, about 250 people were still standing in line. It was almost midnight when the smiling yet exhausted couple finally shook the last hand and signed the last autograph. It was not the first time they had done that. But they were happy to do it because they always feel a deep sense of gratitude to their fans. To them, it's all part of the job.

When we returned to their home in Iowa after a grueling five days on the road, Lee and Tiffany were eager to shoot their bows. Hunting season was not far off, and they wanted to get in as much practice as possible. Before leaving on the trip, Lee had set up a 3-D course in the woods behind his house, but he hadn't had a chance to shoot it. The targets consisted of an elk, several deer, an antelope and several other life-size critters, each placed in the woods in natural settings to simulate real hunting conditions.

Shooting a brand-new Mathews bow that he would be hunting with in 2011, Lee dialed in his sight and consistently hit the elk target in the kill zone at 100 yards. I was blown away. Then he proceeded to shoot the antelope target and a mule deer target at 60 to 80 yards. Tiffany consistently shot several of the targets at 65 to 70 yards. Every arrow was in the kill zone.

When it comes to bow-hunting, knowing their equipment and knowing their quarry, Lee and Tiffany are truly professionals in every sense of the word. They are the real thing.

I have known several very wise old men who have achieved amazing success in their lives, and they've all pretty much stated a kind of truth I will always remember. In essence, they said that as they look back on their lives and the succession of events that helped them fulfill their dreams, it almost reads like the chapters in a book that someone had written long before they started their uncertain journey. It was almost like some unknown force wrote out a script for their life journeys before those journeys actually began. And that script was somehow followed to a T, even though these men didn't know at the time they were walking that road.

You could say the same thing about Lee and Tiffany, except for two things. First, they are not old timers; they are still practically kids. And second, they never set out to gain any kind of recognition or become the most famous personalities in the hunting industry. It simply happened.

All they ever set out to do was to enjoy their passion for hunting and to be together. Everything else has been icing on the cake. Certainly, their stars must have been lined up just right, because everything they have done has propelled them into the limelight and led to the incredible recognition they enjoy today. And no one deserves it more.

But like all things, recognition and fame do not come without a price. As my good friend David Blanton of Realtree recently said, "They have handled their fame with a grace and dignity like no one else I have ever known in the industry. As personalities come and go in the hunting world, if we can continue to produce celebrities with the same values as Lee and Tiffany, our industry will benefit tremendously, and it will always be respected. They are the greatest ambassadors to the sport of deer hunting I have ever known."

CHAPTER 1

AN AMAZING SUCCESS STORY

For as long as he can remember, Lee Lakosky was infatuated with whitetails.

"My dad, Leonard Lakosky, and my uncles went deer hunting every season," Lee said. "They were mainly meat hunters, like most people back in those days. Whenever they were lucky enough to come home with a deer — usually a doe, if they got anything at all — I would spend hours sitting beside the carcass — or sometimes on it — studying every feature of that deer. If it was a small buck, after they hung it in my grandfather's barn, I would pretend to shoot it with my cap gun about 600,000 times, killing it over and over again in my imagination. My dad was a bricklayer, and we were just a blue-collar family.

"Tiffany and I do a lot of seminars each year, and one of the most frequent comments we get is, 'I can't believe you pass up some of the deer that you pass up every season.' Sometimes we can't believe it either, but it wasn't always that way. To be quite honest, it wasn't too many years ago that if I shot a spike, I'd be driving around with it in my truck for two weeks. Well, not literally, but it sure seems like it.

Leonard Lakosky, Lee's dad, poses with a big-bodied 8-pointer from northern Minnesota taken in the early 1970s. Note that the deer's neck had been cut, a common practice in those days to properly "bleed out" a deer. The barn in the background, belonging to Lee's grandfather, is where all the deer taken by family members were hung and butchered.

A proud Lee shows off his first buck, taken in November 1982. Lee shot the young 8-pointer with a Winchester .30-30 on opening weekend of the Minnesota season. He was 16.

"I grew up in the city of Minneapolis, and I could see the IDS Tower right from my bedroom window. I didn't know anybody with any hunting property, and no one in my family owned any property, so it wasn't like my family had any great places to hunt. But all of my relatives came from northern Minnesota, and that's where my dad and all of my uncles hunted when they were growing up. So it became a tradition for us to go up there in the fall.

"We hunted in the Superior National Forest, and there were no food plots, no fields and very few deer. I started deer hunting when I was 9, but I didn't shoot my first deer until I was 16

Here's Lee pheasant hunting with his dad in North Dakota in the late 1980s. Although Lee grew up hunting ducks and pheasants with his dad and several good friends, whitetails always held a special fascination for him.

Here's Lee's second deer with a bow, a doe, taken in the late 1980s. His first deer with a bow, also a doe, was taken about 1986, when he was 20. "I got interested in bow-hunting when I was about 13, but it still took me a long time to get my first doe with a bow," Lee said.

years old. Actually, I couldn't legally hunt until I was 12, but I tagged along with my dad as much as I could before that. During those seven or eight years, I bet we didn't see a dozen deer the whole time. There just weren't very many in those days. Dad would sit all day, and sometimes when nothing was happening, he'd let me shoot a squirrel with my .410.

"The deer population in that area might be a little higher now, but back then, by the second weekend of the season, we always hunted in waist-deep snow, and there were lots of wolves around. The first deer I shot was actually the first buck I ever saw. He was a little basket-racked 8, and when I got him, I could have died and gone to heaven.

"Everyone in my family hunted deer, small game and birds, but I don't remember any one person having an overwhelming influence on my interest in deer and deer hunting. It was just something that I always wanted to do. I did a lot of hunting and

This is Lee's first buck with a bow (circa 1988). When Lee shot this yearling 6-pointer at age 22, little could he imagine what the future would hold for him. During the next two decades, he would grow to be one of America's best-known bow-hunters, with dozens of exceptional bucks to his credit.

When Lee's diehard hunting companion Paul Landberg, left, shot this Minnesota monster in the late 1980s, it changed the way the hunters felt about chasing big whitetails. "From that day forward, everything else took a back seat to whitetail hunting, and I wasn't going to rest until I shot a deer like that myself," Lee said. Pictured with Paul and Lee is Paul's dad, center.

trapping with my grandfather in northern Minnesota, but we seldom saw any deer.

"My grandparents' house was located on the outskirts of town, and my grandfather had an old mounted deer in his basement. Every time I went to visit there, the first thing I did was run downstairs to the basement and stare at that deer. I was spellbound. And this was long before I was old enough to hunt. When I was about 5 years old, I remember sitting by the window and waiting for all my relatives to get back from a hunt. It seemed like I would sit there for hours, and 90 percent of the time, they came home empty-handed. My grandfather always had a big stack of *Outdoor Life* and *Field & Stream* magazines, and I would look through the pages and drool over the pictures of deer for hours on end.

"I was always fascinated with deer. Tiffany has even asked me how I could be so obsessed with deer and deer hunting at such a young age after I had hunted for all those years and seldom even seen a deer. Maybe that's why.

"I would look in the magazines and see pictures of all those big deer other people were shooting, and I figured I must be doing something wrong. You'd see scrapes, and you'd see rubs up where we hunted, but we never saw any of the bucks that made them. I often thought, 'Man, if I could just get one of these guys

Lee arrowed his first Pope and Young buck in 1994. The big Minnesota 9-pointer grossed 150 inches.

Lee's 1994 buck was a mature, heavy-framed 4-by-5 with a split G-2. The rack netted about 134 inches.

who writes all the articles about deer hunting to come up here, maybe he could show me how to do it.' The men who wrote the stories in those magazines were magical to me. They knew it all.

"I've always been very stubborn, and maybe that has been a good thing through the years. I figured the deer had to be there, but I just didn't know how to hunt them. That stubborn streak made me more determined than ever to learn, no matter how long it took. It wasn't until I shot my first buck at 16 when things started to turn around.

"I started doing a lot of hunting with a good friend, Paul Landberg, a neighbor who grew up four doors down from me. There was a Holiday Food Store not far from us that had a huge sporting goods and hunting section (it's a Gander Mountain now), and we would visit it on weekends or whenever we could. They were open 24 hours, and sometimes we would go there at 2 a.m. to buy shells when we were going duck hunting.

"When some of the first deer hunting videos started coming out, like *King of the North* with Curt Gowdy in the mid-1980s, we would rent those videos and spend every night on the weekends watching them and drooling over some of those big bucks. We watched videos with people like Tom Miranda and Dan Fitzgerald, and we got enthralled with deer hunting and the idea of shooting big bucks.

"Paul was a year older than me, and when he turned 16, our whole world changed. That meant he could drive, and our hunting horizons expanded dramatically. Paul and I are still very good friends to this day, and we still hunt together every season.

"Even though we lived in the city, we didn't have to go that far to find good places to hunt on the outskirts of town, seldom more than about 30 miles from home. By then, I had gotten very interested in bow-hunting, and just about any landowner you asked would let you bow-hunt on their property. Bow-hunting

The pinnacle of Lee's early bow-hunting career came in December 1995, when he shot his biggest buck ever, a Minnesota giant that netted 177 inches. To date, the buck is still the largest typical whitetail he's ever taken.

Lee shot this beautiful 135-inch buck on an abandoned government installation known locally as the Arsenal. Well-known outdoor writer Gary Clancy used Lee's photo to illustrate his book *Advanced Whitetail Hunting*, published in 1996.

was still sort of a new thing, and most landowners considered it a lot safer than gun-hunting, so it was easy getting permission.

"I got interested in bow-hunting when I was about 13, but it still took me a long time — seven long years to be exact — to get my first doe with a bow. I think I was 20 at the time. That would have been around 1986. The first bow I had was a Browning Nomad compound with laminated wooden limbs. It was beautiful. Paul and I would go out and knock on doors, and most landowners who deer hunted during gun season thought bow-hunting was a novelty. They'd give you a strange look and say, 'You're going to try to shoot one with a bow and arrow? Yeah, go ahead.'

"We found a lot of places to hunt, but we didn't know anything about deer hunting, and we didn't have anyone to show us how to do it. So everything we did was by trial and error. The first buck I ever shot with a bow was a small 6-pointer a year or two after I shot my doe. I was probably 22. Looking back, that doesn't seem so long ago.

An Obsession with Deer Hunting

"Today, I always find it very ironic that whenever Tiffany and I are at a deer show somewhere, little kids about 8 or 9 years old will frequently come up to us and show us pictures of giant bucks they've taken. It took me a lot longer than that to get my first good deer and to really make any progress in my deer hunting career. But after I shot my first buck with a bow, I wanted something bigger and better, and my hunting career started progressing fairly rapidly.

"Eventually, Paul and I found a place to hunt within the city limits of Minneapolis that had been closed to hunting for a long time. Paul's dad happened to be a friend of one of the city council members, and we had heard that a certain section of land was going to be opened up to bow-hunting because the deer were getting overpopulated. We went and talked to some of the landowners, and they all told us, 'You can't deer hunt here. It's not legal.' But we told them we thought it was going to be open pretty soon. Actually, we had a head start on everyone else because we were so in tune with what was going on in the area.

"Every day during the summer, we were out looking at deer and knocking on doors, offering to bale hay or milk cows for the landowners, and every day we were shooting our bows and looking for spots to hunt. And we found some pretty good spots. Today, I often think about the fact that if I knew then what I know now about hunting mature bucks, we no doubt would have taken some incredible deer. Since everything we hunted was inside the city limits, no gun-hunting was allowed, and I'm sure there were some real giants around. But we never saw them.

"Paul and his dad had a place to hunt in the city limits that was owned by one of their relatives. At the time, we each had taken a few small bucks — mostly forkies — but neither of us had ever seen a racked buck while actually hunting. One day, Paul was hunting on his relative's farm just down from where I was hunting when he came and picked me up. 'I think I just hit a pretty good buck,' he said.

"He didn't really know how big the deer was. When it came through, he saw that it had a rack, and he simply aimed his bow and shot it. So we went back to the spot and searched for hours with flashlights. Around midnight, I thought I smelled something similar to what you smell when you're gutting a deer. I turned and walked a short distance, and bang, there it was. It was an absolute monster. It was the biggest deer I had ever seen, living or dead, and it took my breath away. 'Oh, my gosh!' I said.

> I turned and walked a short distance, and bang, there it was. It was an absolute monster. It was the biggest deer I had ever seen, living or dead, and it took my breath away. "Oh, my gosh!" I said.

"The moment Paul saw it, we were jumping up and down and going crazy. It was a huge 10-pointer, and it grossed more than 170 inches. Up to that point, Paul and I had religiously duck hunted, grouse hunted and pheasant hunted together, but after I saw that deer, it was like a light bulb went on in my head. Even though I had never shot a deer like that myself, I wasn't going to rest until I did. From that day on, every other kind of hunting took a back seat to whitetail hunting. Bird hunting got shuffled off to the side unless I filled my deer tags early. I was determined to shoot a big deer.

"My big day came several years later in 1994. Paul and I found a good spot to hunt out in Scandia, Minn., just north of Forest Lake. We were learning more and more each season about how to hunt whitetails, and that's where I shot my first Pope and Young buck. He was a mature, heavy framed 4-by-5 with a split G2, and he grossed 150 inches. He netted around 134.

"The next year, 1995, we got permission to hunt on a 10-acre tract in Blaine, Minn., that hadn't been hunted in 13 years. The land was next to a state park, and five acres of it was the part that the owner's house was on, so we were basically hunting on

When three small bucks stepped out on the afternoon of Sept. 24, 1999, there was no doubt that Tiffany was going to become a very competent bow-hunter. She made a perfect shot on the last deer in a line, thus embarking on a career that would produce many outstanding whitetails.

the back five acres. The back five acres had a little four-wheeler track around it that was always planted in clover. The owner would mow the clover with a riding lawnmower, and the local deer would come out of the park and feed on the clover.

"Paul and I had each bought a new compound bow — PSE Mock Flight 4 compounds. That year, Paul had already tagged out with a good deer, so I was hunting alone. It was in later December just before Christmas. I had read stories and heard a lot about the secondary rut that occurs in late December, but I had never experienced it firsthand. I was hunting over that little clover plot when a doe suddenly ran out into the open.

"Two bucks were chasing her. Both deer were very nice bucks. One was a huge 10, and the other was a slightly smaller 8. The doe ran right past me. The big 8 ran right out into the open and stopped well out of range, but the big 10 was a lot more cautious. He stopped in the edge of the clearing about 45 yards away and would not step out into the open.

"It was a long shot, but Paul and I had been practicing every day. After the shot, the buck ran off and disappeared behind some brush. The doe and the other buck walked over to the spot where the big 10 had disappeared. Suddenly, they both perked up as if to say, 'What the heck is that?' and they bolted off. I saw two tails waving instead of three, and I thought, 'Maybe I got him.'

"I walked over to the spot where I had last seen him. There was a lot of snow on the ground, and it was very cold. He was propped up against a bush in the snow, and when I got a good look at both of his antlers, I couldn't believe it. He was huge. I almost fell over. That moment is still one of the most exciting moments I've ever had while hunting. It gives me goose bumps just to talk about it now. He was a huge buck with a beautiful rack that netted 177 inches. To this day, he's still the largest typical whitetail that I've ever taken in my life. So for two years in a row, I was very fortunate to shoot two really good deer.

"In order to get to that point, though, it had taken me years of learning how to hunt. I made plenty of mistakes, and I had to learn how to control my emotions before the shot. Even today, I still get buck fever when I see a good deer. Your heart starts pounding, your knees start shaking, but you learn to control it.

"After that, the city of Minneapolis started a program called the Metro Resource Base, in which it offered bow-hunts inside the city limits. You had to take a bow-hunter safety course, but when you got certified, you could go into a lot of places where the city wanted to remove some deer. I didn't get one the first year, but the second year I shot a pretty good buck that scored 135 inches in the Arsenal, a place we hunted in Arden Hills.

"The Arsenal was an old government military installation that had been closed down. In fact, well-known outdoor writer Gary Clancy used a photo of my buck on the cover of a book he did about bow-hunting titled *Advanced Whitetail Hunting*, published in 1996. I was thrilled.

Expanded Horizons

"By the late '90s, Paul and I were in our early 30s, and we finally figured out that if we were ever going to shoot any trophy deer on a consistent basis, we'd have to go somewhere else to do it. So every weekend, we started driving down to Iowa and sometimes to Kansas just to look at deer.

"We had read stories about how big these Midwestern deer were, and we had to see it for ourselves. When we first started going to Iowa, nonresidents couldn't even hunt there, but we went just to look at all the deer out in the fields. We were blown away. We had never seen anything like it. We'd go around in the evenings and see 30 or 40 deer in a single alfalfa or bean field. That never happened in Minnesota.

"I didn't know a soul in either of those states at the time or even the best places to go, but we would read about all the big bucks coming out of Kansas and Iowa in *North American Whitetail*, which was our bible. And while our friends back home were going to bars and parties on the weekends, we'd be in the car looking for deer in Iowa and trying to line up some spots to hunt, because we knew Iowa would eventually open up hunting to nonresidents.

"Later, when that first season opened in Iowa, we never even had to apply for the draw. There were nearly 500 leftover tags. So we started hunting on public land, and every year, we'd usually bring home at least one good Pope and Young buck.

"During the 1990s, I worked at an archery pro shop in Little Canada, Minn., called Bwana Archery Shop, owned by John Larsen. Every fall, he would hire me as a bow tech, and I would help people set up their bows. I was a fanatic about all the equipment and setting up bows the right way, and I loved doing it.

> By the late '90s, Paul and I were in our early 30s, and we finally figured out that if we were ever going to shoot any trophy deer on a consistent basis, we'd have to go somewhere else to do it.

Pretty soon, everyone got to know me, and I was setting up bows for dozens of people. Even today, I have a shop at home complete with bow presses and everything else I need to work on bows, and every year I still set up a lot of bows for my friends.

"By the time I was 25 in the early '90s, I was hunting all the time, working at the archery shop in the fall or doing odd jobs like painting during the off season. I loved what I was doing, but all of my friends were graduating from college, getting jobs and buying houses. All I ever wanted to do was hunt. Even my sister came to me one day and said, 'You're never going to do anything with your life because all you ever think about is deer hunting.'"

Lee's sister was only partly right. Yes, he was obsessed with deer hunting, but he also had ambitions and dreams, and he was

Even though he had arrowed some big bucks in his native Minnesota during the mid-'90s, Lee knew he had to expand his horizons. He shot this outstanding 10-pointer while hunting in Kansas during 1998.

willing to do whatever it took to achieve those dreams. At 25, one of his fondest dreams was to own some hunting land in a good area that he could manage for big bucks. He knew he had to buckle down and get a college degree to get the kind of job that would allow him to reach his goals. So he started attending the University of Minnesota-Duluth.

When he applied himself, Lee did extremely well in college. In fact, he did so well in math, chemistry and physics that he tutored other students all the way through school. And typical of the way he always planned his life around his fall deer hunting schedule, his grades were so good that he was able to arrange his classes or even skip classes when necessary to accommodate deer season. So even with a busy college schedule, Lee was still able to beat the system and hunt just about every morning and evening during deer season.

All I ever wanted to do was hunt.

Lee earned his initial degree in economics. Then, realizing how good he had it during his college days and not yet ready to get a real job — he was afraid a job might curtail his sacred hunting schedule in fall — he went back to the university and earned a second degree in chemical engineering.

A Different Kind of Arrow Affliction

Throughout his college career, Lee had worked at the archery shop. It was there, while getting his second degree, that a beautiful, blond-haired, 18-year-old high-school graduate with a bubbly personality named Tiffany Profant caught his eye. He and Tiffany had actually known each other for a long time. She and one of Lee's sisters had been good friends for at least five years, so Lee had known Tiffany since she was about 12 or 13 years old. (Lee has five sisters and one brother.) Of course, at the time he first met her, Lee was about 20, and Tiffany had just reached her teen years. Although she was already eye-catching as a young teen-ager, she was much too young to consider dating.

But when they met later, things were noticeably different. Tiffany had grown up into a beautiful young woman. Ironically, at the time Lee went back to the University of Minnesota to earn his second degree in chemical engineering, she was just starting college there.

"So we would see each other around school during her freshman year, and we started hanging out and going out on a few dates," Lee said. "Tiffany is so likable, and she has such a wonderful personality that everyone in the archery shop just loved her, and pretty soon we had her fletching arrows with us and coming by the shop on a regular basis.

"Several years went by, and she had become an archery shop regular. Then one day out of the clear blue, I asked her if she would like to try shooting a bow. Being the adventurous type who is always willing to try almost anything, she said, 'Sure.' But since Tiffany is so small, we had a problem because we couldn't find a bow small enough to fit her.

"Nobody was making bows for women at the time. She only had a 23-inch draw, and even back then, we couldn't find anything that would work other than a kid's bow. I didn't want her shooting anything that I wouldn't shoot, but about that time, PSE came out with a Mini G that was basically a small men's bow with a 25-inch draw (the shortest draw length available at that time). So that's what we got her. It came with 60-pound limbs, and we short-strung it to take some of the weight off and added 70-pound limbs. That way, she ended up with the 23-inch draw length that she needed. She was pulling about 50 pounds, and it worked very well for her.

"While I was working, she'd be over on the indoor range shooting away. All the pro shooters were always practicing, and naturally they took a real liking to her. They worked with her, and pretty soon she became a super-good shot.

"I never thought that she'd ever have any interest in hunting. For the first two years we dated, I would always take off during hunting season and be gone for nearly the whole month of November. By now, I was pushing 30, and Tiffany was around 22, and she had become a flight attendant with Northwest Airlines. So whenever I left to go hunting, she and her mom would fly to Hawaii for a week of relaxation."

Several years earlier, during her first year of attending the university, tragedy had struck Tiffany's family. At 43, her dad, Gary, a Vietnam veteran who was always in great physical condition and the picture of good health, died suddenly and unexpectedly from a heart attack. Only a few weeks before he died, Tiffany's mom, Linda, had been diagnosed with breast cancer and needed a mastectomy. At 18 years old, Tiffany was faced with the possibility of losing both her parents.

So she dropped out of school during her freshman year and came home to help her mom get through the surgery and the follow-up chemotherapy. Much to her regret, Tiffany never returned to school. Instead, she got a job with Northwest Airlines as soon as her mother seemed to be on the road to recovery. That probably proved to be best for her in the long run. Because of her looks and personality, being a flight attendant was the perfect job for her. Linda went on to beat cancer, and today she has been cancer-free for many years.

A Hunter is Born

"Eventually, Tiffany and I started flying all over the Midwest, exploring new areas and looking for good places to hunt," Lee said. "During the summer, we'd fly to places like Denver and rent a car and drive to eastern Colorado or up to Nebraska to look at certain spots in the southwestern corner by the Republican River, where some big deer had been killed. She just had that personality and that adventurous spirit, and she was willing to do just about anything that I wanted to do. If I said something like, 'Let's go skydiving tomorrow,' she'd say, 'Sure, that would be great. Let's go do it,' and she would do it without batting an eye.

"Sometimes, I'd drive down from Minneapolis to Kansas or southern Iowa to check out a certain area, and Tiffany would fly down and join me a day or two later. In those days, we knocked on a lot of doors and talked to a lot of people, asking permission to bow-hunt. I didn't know anybody, and I certainly didn't have any connections. But we had a lot of determination. Through trial and error, and the process of elimination, we found some great places to hunt. In those early days, we hunted on a lot of public land. You'd be surprised how good some of it was.

"So after we had been traveling all across Kansas and Iowa and other places, I finally just asked her one day, 'Would you like to try hunting?' She said, 'Sure, why not?' Up until that time, she'd been going with me, and actually sitting in a tree with me and helping me video. So when I asked her if she wanted to go hunting, she said, 'I don't know if I can actually kill anything, but I guess I'll try it.'

"She was already a very good shot with a bow because of her experience at the archery shop. We'd also been shooting in 3-D tournaments with all of my buddies, and she always beat half of them. So right from the beginning, we got her outfitted with good equipment that fit her. She had all the pro shooters teaching her how to shoot with back tension, and I knew she wouldn't have any problem making the shot. She had that part down. However, I knew that if she were going to have a problem, it would be in the killing part.

"The first time we went out, we went to my spot in Scandia, and three little bucks came out. She was a little nervous, and she wasn't completely comfortable in that tree, and just before the three bucks appeared, she whispered, 'I don't know if I can shoot anything.'

"She'd been in a tree with me quite a bit filming with the video camera, but this was different because now she had to draw her bow in the tree, and that was a little more difficult to do. I was sitting just above her, and she was wearing her safety belt, of course, and her shoulders were between my knees, and I tried to make sure she was steady. I had set up her tree stand so that she could shoot from a sitting position.

"After those first three bucks came out, however, there was no doubt that she was going to shoot one of them. She was so excited. But at the same time, she was very calm. 'I'm shooting. I'm shooting,' she whispered. There was no question that she could do it.

"By the time the third buck came by at about 25 yards, she was still very calm, and I started talking her through it. 'Use your 25-yard pin, draw back slowly, make sure you have your anchor point, burn that pin on that buck's shoulder and just squeeze the trigger.'

"She was a perfect student as I walked her through it, and she absolutely smoked that buck. He was a nice young 6-pointer, and he ran about 30 yards out into an alfalfa field and dropped right there. She was still so excited. If you think she gets excited now on television with big mature bucks, you should have seen her after she shot her first little yearling buck. She was jumping up and down and calling everybody she knew. She called my dad and her mom and everyone at the archery shop. And everyone was so excited for her.

"The next year, we went out to the same tree in the same spot at Scandia, and it was a repeat of the year before, only this time her second deer was a slightly larger 6-pointer. That year, I had also gotten her tags to bow-hunt with me in Iowa and Kansas, and she shot a beautiful 10-pointer in Iowa that scored about 130. In Kansas, she shot a very old buck with a big body. He probably scored around 140 inches, and he easily could have been 9 or 10 years old. She was so excited to get that old buck.

"On each of those hunts, we had always hunted together, and I was always in the tree with her. We were never apart in separate trees, because it was something that we wanted to do together. And I always had the camera and filmed every hunt just for fun. By that time, I was so totally into deer hunting that a friend of mine, Jim Hill, put me in touch with Gordon Whittington at *North American Whitetail*. Gordon encouraged me to write some articles for the magazine. So I started writing a few articles for *North American Whitetail* during the off-season when I wasn't hunting, and I did a few for *Deer and Deer Hunting* as well.

> If I said something like, "Let's go skydiving tomorrow," Tiffany would say, "Sure, that would be great. Let's go do it," and she would do it without batting an eye.

GOING FOR BROKE

"As a result of my story writing, I was able to get a media pass to the Archery Trade Association show held in Indianapolis in January 2000," Lee said. "I was so excited to be able to go to that show because archery was my passion, and seeing and meeting some of the manufacturers, dealers and other bow-hunters there was a huge thrill. For me, it was like being a young kid and going to the circus for the first time."

Lee graduated from college with his chemical engineering degree in 1999 and went to work as a chemical engineer for Koch Oil Refinery south of Minneapolis. He took the job — on his own terms, of course — only because he learned that the company was offering a new position in which certain people in management could work a 12-hour shift just like the people who worked in the refinery. Engineers such as Lee were always being called in at night to solve various problems, so the company decided to have shifts of engineers working at night to have someone available around the clock when needed.

In Lee's case, it was a perfect arrangement, and he probably wouldn't have taken the job under any other conditions. Each

During their first year of attempting to videotape hunts for professional videos such as *Realtree's Monster Bucks* series in 2001, Lee and Tiffany had one of their best seasons ever. Tiffany shot a beautiful 147-inch 8-pointer in Kansas and a very old buck in Wisconsin that she was thrilled to get. Lee shot three huge bucks: a 196-inch nontypical giant in Kansas, pictured above; a massive 174-inch 10-pointer in Iowa, pictured on Page 42; and a 170-inch brute in Wisconsin, pictured on Page 41.

month, he worked a shift of three days on, two off, then three on and three off, and then four on and seven off. That worked out so he had seven consecutive days off every month. That precious week of time was always used to go to Kansas and Iowa to look for land, watch deer and prepare for hunting season.

Just as he had done in college, Lee essentially manipulated the system to his benefit because his time in the woods was so vitally important to him. When hunting season rolled around, he would combine his 14 days of vacation with the seven days off. Using that time off, including weekends, he could take off all of November to hunt.

He would leave to go hunting in Kansas and Iowa on Oct. 25, and he didn't have to be back at work until about Dec. 3. Actually, when you're as obsessed with something as much as Lee was obsessed with deer hunting, it would have been easy for him to rationalize that his real full-time job was deer hunting. Working for the refinery was simply a part-time inconvenience and a necessary evil required to pay the bills.

A Close Call for Tiffany

Lee was at work one day in December 1999 just before Christmas when Tiffany's mom called and told him that Tiffany was in the hospital. He left work and drove to the hospital as quickly as possible. Tiffany had just returned from a routine trip to Japan as a flight attendant for Northwest Airlines, and her mom, Linda, was working at Cub Foods making fruits baskets for the holidays. Tiffany had been talking to a friend when she suddenly started feeling very strange. Her arms became numb, and she had difficulty breathing. Linda immediately drove her to the hospital, where doctors soon discovered that Tiffany had suffered a small stroke.

Apparently, many babies are born with small holes in their hearts. But in more than 70 percent of the cases, the holes close up naturally as the baby gets older. Even with the other 30 percent, the small hole is seldom a problem. But in Tiffany's case, that small heart defect made a blood clot form in her lungs. The clot went to her brain and caused a stroke. It could have been a lot worse.

Tiffany soon learned that she would have to undergo open-heart surgery to repair the hole

Here's Lee's 174-inch Iowa megabuck, which he rattled in while Tiffany ran the camera. This buck was featured on the back cover of Realtree's *Monster Bucks 10* video.

in her heart. The surgery went well, and while recuperating, she was grounded from flying anywhere for several weeks. So 10 days after she had her open-heart surgery, she attended what would be the couple's first ATA Show in Indianapolis with Lee.

"She told her mom, 'Yep, I'm going to the show,' Lee said. "Naturally, Linda wasn't too happy about us going. And since Tiffany couldn't fly, we got in the car and drove to Indianapolis. What a trip it turned out to be. The show was tailor-made for me since I had become such an archery nut. I was so thrilled to see all of the manufacturers and their products. Everything and everyone at that show caught my attention.

"Tiffany and I actually got to meet so many other well-known people in the hunting industry for the first time. We met all the guys from Realtree, including Bill Jordan, Michael

Waddell and David Blanton. We also met Ashley Snipes, who was the pro staff director at Realtree. I really hit it off well with Michael. At that time, he was a cameraman for Realtree. That was just before he got so popular in shows like *Road Trips* and *Bone Collector*, but I had already seen him in some of Realtree's *Monster Bucks* videos, and I had a lot of respect for his hunting abilities. We became really good friends after that.

"We met other well-known industry people at show, like Mark and Terry Drury, Jay and Tammi Gregory, and Don and Kandi Kisky. It was such an honor to meet all of those people. To me, they were all icons in the business. In fact, Tiffany and I were about the same age as a lot of the young hunting couples that were getting so popular, like Jay and Tammi, Don and Kandi, and individuals like Michael Waddell, and we started hanging out with them on a regular basis.

> Michael Waddell said, "With the kind of bucks you're shooting every year, you ought to start filming some hunts for our *Monster Bucks* series."

"Since I now had a real job with Koch, I had just bought my first piece of land down in Kansas. It was a place I had been hunting for several years, and I had shot some really nice bucks on it. It was a big piece, 1,000 acres located near Junction City. I couldn't afford to buy it by myself, so I went in with one of the guys at the refinery and one of his buddies, Tom Roles, who later became one of my best friends and a partner in several other farms.

"Since Tiffany and I had hit it off with Michael and the other folks at Realtree so well, Ashley Snipes asked us to be on Realtree's local pro staff and do some appearances with Michael that fall at several Cabela's stores. Tiffany and I were deeply honored.

Breaking into Video

"Michael, of course, was a huge turkey hunter, and when I told him we had lots of turkeys on our Kansas property, he said, 'Let's go hunt them next year.' I had never hunted turkeys before. Growing up in Minnesota, we didn't have many, and there were none in northern Minnesota in the areas we deer hunted (though all that has changed now). So in Spring 2000, Michael, Ashley — who soon became his wife — and John Tate, another well-known cameraman with Realtree, came down to our farm in Kansas to hunt turkeys and do some filming for Realtree's video series *All-Stars of Spring*.

"By that time, I had shot several good bucks — my 177 typical in Minnesota, a couple of 140s in Iowa and a couple of good bucks in Kansas. Michael said, 'With the kind of bucks you're shooting every year, you ought to start filming some hunts for our *Monster Bucks* series.'

In 2000, Lee and Tiffany attended the Archery Trade Association show and met several well-known hunting industry professionals, such as David Blanton of Realtree, left.

"I said, 'Oh my gosh, that would be a dream of mine.'

"While we were turkey hunting, John Tate gave me a lot of great pointers on how to use a camera, and how to film cutaways and recoveries. We were filming turkey hunts, but that was OK. I still learned a lot. So I went out and bought a Canon XL1 and some wireless microphones, and the next season, Tiffany and I were in the video business. We went out determined to try to film some of our hunts as professionally as possible.

"As things turned out, we had the best season ever. That year, 2001, I shot a 170 in Wisconsin, a 174 in Iowa and a 196 in Kansas. Tiffany shot a 147-inch 8-pointer in Kansas and a deer that scored in the mid-130s in Wisconsin. Amazingly, our footage was really good, especially since it was the first time we had ever attempted to film an entire hunt from start to finish that could be used in a professional video. For Tiffany, it was the first time she had ever been behind the camera trying to film a complete hunt. She had filmed deer out in a field with a video camera while we sat in a tree together, but this was the first time

In 2001, Don and Kandi Kisky did a video with Mark and Terry Drury called *Whitetails, Taking it to the Extreme*. They used Lee and Tiffany's footage of Lee's 196-inch Kansas buck and two of Tiffany's hunts.

During the 2003 season, Lee and Tiffany started filming for their first TV show, *Gettin' Close with Lee and Tiffany*.

that either of us had ever tried to film a complete hunt.

"We were so fortunate because David Blanton ended putting my 174-inch buck on the back cover of *Monster Bucks 10*. After that happened, I thought I had died and gone to heaven. I had always been such a huge fan of the *Monster Bucks* series. Paul and I owned every deer hunting video Realtree had ever produced, and Tiffany and I were so thrilled to be a part of one of their videos now. We did it purely for the fun of doing it, and we never even thought about asking for any money or even trying to make any money doing it.

"That same year (2001), Don and Kandi Kisky were doing a video with Mark and Terry Drury called *Whitetails, Taking It To the Extreme*. In that video, they used the footage we had shot of the 196-inch buck I had taken in Kansas, as well as two of Tiffany's hunts.

"The next year (2002), we had another great year, and we did it all over again. Once again, we never tried to make any money filming any of our hunts, we never planned to have a TV show, and we never dreamed that we might become popular deer hunting personalities. We just did it because we loved doing it so much and because we loved being a part of something so special to us. It was fun to do, and ever since I had started hunting with Paul years earlier, we had watched just about every deer hunting video ever made.

2011 marked the fourth season of Lee and Tiffany's top-rated television program *The Crush*.

Iowa Bound: Fields of Many Dreams

"About that same time, the management at the refinery began making some changes. I was told that I couldn't work a shift any more, and the company started clamping down on me about all the time I had been taking off to hunt during fall. Tiffany and I were spending more and more time on the go, hunting and filming together each season, and I can't tell you how depressing it was to think about not being able to hunt as much as I had been used to doing during October and November.

"I managed to do all right as the summer progressed, but when Oct. 1 rolled around, it was decision time. After worrying myself sick about my fall hunting schedule all summer long and doing a lot of soul-searching, I walked into work and told my bosses that I was through working at the refinery. I told them, 'This isn't what I want to do. I'm not happy doing it, and I'm done.' So I quit that day.

"I met Tiffany for lunch later on, and she said, 'Why aren't you at work?'

"I answered, 'I just quit.'

"We had just gotten married on Aug. 23, 2003. We had taken our honeymoon out in Wyoming at the 7 J Ranch hunting with David Blanton and John Tate (see Chapter 15), and the thought of not being able to do what I had always loved doing for so many years was overwhelming. Spending time with David on that hunt was a huge turning point in my career. It made me realize what the potential was for getting into the outdoor industry, and it gave me the confidence I needed to quit my job. Having a good job had allowed me to buy that first piece of property in Kansas, but I just couldn't picture myself working at that refinery for the next 30 years.

"After I quit, I had no idea what I was going to do. It was early October, and the 2003 hunting season was just starting. In addition to the tract I owned in Kansas, I had just bought an interest in a small farm in Iowa. A friend of mine who worked for UPS in Minnesota had a customer on his route that told him, 'Hey, my aunt has some property she wants to sell in Salem, Iowa.'

"So we bought it. And it just happens to be the piece where our house sits now. It was 280 acres. It's a phenomenal piece of land. Three of us — me, my UPS buddy and another friend — went in and bought it together.

"We had just started to build a small cabin on the property to use as a hunting cabin, and I said to Tiffany, 'Let's move to Iowa.'

"Even though I had no idea what I was going to do for a living, I knew that I planned to be hunting the entire season, and it made sense to live in Iowa. There were several big chemical plants in eastern Iowa, and I figured that if worse came to worse, I could get a job as an engineer at one of those plants. Because she worked for Northwest, Tiffany could live anywhere. If we moved to Iowa, she could easily commute back and forth from Des Moines or Cedar Rapids to Minneapolis, where she was based. So I quit my job on Oct. 1, and two days later, we had packed up the few possessions we owned and were headed to Iowa.

"I didn't want to do any hunting without having Tiffany film for me, so she arranged her schedule so that she would have plenty of time off. By then, she had been working for Northwest for about 10 years, and she had built up some seniority. She started working some five-day trips to Japan so that she would have a week or 10 days off when she returned.

"One afternoon in mid-October, I was over at Don and Kandi Kisky's, helping them combine their corn. Tiffany and I had become very good friends with them, and their farm was about two hours away from where we lived. Out of the clear blue, Aubrey Gale at Scent-Lok called me on my cell phone and said, 'We're thinking about doing another TV show. Would you and Tiffany be interested in hosting it?'

"I was a little tongue-tied, but I answered, 'Well, Aubrey, the timing is pretty good. I just quit my job, and we just moved down here to Iowa. If we can do it the way we want to do it, yes, we'd be very interested.'

"I had never thought about doing a TV show. I was very nervous about it, because I had always been very particular about the way I did things, and I didn't want the show to be a disaster. Above all else, I didn't want it to be a show with an agenda or

> We had just started to build a small cabin on the property to use as a hunting cabin, and I said to Tiffany, "Let's move to Iowa."

an infomercial for Scent-Lok. They said, 'You can do it any way you want.'

"Having been such a big fan of other videos and other shows that were now on TV, I felt like I knew a lot about what it took to make a good show. I knew what I wanted to see, and I figured that since I was such an avid deer hunter, the viewers out there would also like the things that I liked.

"So during the 2003 season, we started filming for the first year of our *Gettin' Close* TV show. From the very start, there was something about Tiffany that people just loved. Even though there were other girls and other husband-and-wife teams hunting on TV, here was a young, cute girl who always wore earrings and who had never hunted before, and suddenly she was shooting all these big bucks.

"Tiffany lit up the Archery Talk website on the internet. Just about every page was about her. Some was good, and some was bad, but everybody had an opinion. I told her, 'If we're gonna do this for a living, you're gonna to have to have thick skin, because a lot of hunters out there have huge egos, and they think they're the best deer hunters around.'

"We decided from the very start that we were going to have fun hunting. That was a priority. We didn't want to act like we were big whitetail authorities and that we knew more than anyone else. Also, we didn't set out to try to teach anybody anything about hunting. We just wanted to go out there, be ourselves and have a good time. In my opinion, the show was going to be a basic reality show with us doing what we had always done. It's like Tiffany had always said anyway: 'We never had a normal date. We were always out looking at deer, or shed hunting or doing something else pertaining to deer. But that's what we wanted to do, and we had fun doing it.'

"And it worked beautifully. There was one small glitch. After we had edited our first episode, Scent-Lok hated it. They said it was too fast-paced and that it would never work. But by the second year, however, we had the highest-rated show in the history of the Outdoor Channel. Personally, I didn't want to do a show like all the other shows on TV. I didn't want to have a show with a five-minute cooking segment and a segment about how to clean your rifle. I wanted to do a show with pure hunting where we were out having fun. And it worked.

"I had just moved to Iowa, and I had recently become a property owner for the first time in my life. Living in Minnesota, all I ever wanted was to live on a dirt road and have fields where I could look at deer out my window and put in some food plots. I had never been on a tractor. I knew nothing about farming or planting food plots when I first moved to Iowa. But I was willing to learn. And I wanted our show to answer questions like, 'How are you going to hunt these deer?' and, 'How are you going to keep them on your property so someone else doesn't shoot them?'

"I wasn't interested in doing a show where we went to an outfitter, and he put us in a tree and we shot a deer. I had never had the money to go to an outfitter in the first place, and I had always done everything myself during all of those formative years. It took me seven years to shoot my first deer with a bow and eight years to shoot one with a gun. I had done it through trial and error.

"Even though it took me a long time, I had figured out a lot of things on my own. Knocking on doors and figuring out what you had to do to shoot that big deer when you did get a good piece of property to hunt — that's what I wanted to show on TV.

"As mentioned, when I was a kid reading all of those stories in *Outdoor Life* and *Field & Stream*, I thought, 'Man, if I could just get the writer who wrote this story to come up to Minnesota and show me how to kill these big deer up here, I'll be well on my way.' In truth, I don't know if anyone could have gone up to northern Minnesota where we hunted in those days and shot a big deer, but I always thought those writers could do anything when it came to hunting. I thought they were gods.

> As a kid, I'd watch the *Jackie Bushman Show* or *Realtree Outdoors*, and I'd say, "Oh my gosh, what a dream to be able to do that," but I never once thought I would ever be doing it myself.

"Through the years, Tiffany and I have hunted with a few outfitters, but 90 percent of our shows depict what we do on our various farms. If you can learn something from watching us put in food plots and seeing how we set up to hunt certain conditions, then that's what I think people want to see. A lot of our success is obviously because of Tiffany, because she has such a great sense of humor, and people love her as a person. And aside from the hunting, she's so funny. She's kept me laughing for the past 15 years. But we always have great footage of great deer in our shows, and people love seeing that as well.

"In truth, we just muddle our way through it like everyone else, but the advantage we have — if there is one — is that we do it 300 days a year. With that much time invested, you do pick up some good stuff along the way. People always say, 'Man, I wish I could shoot a deer like that.'

"And I always tell them, 'If you hunt the same buck for 100 days a year on a good farm you will,' but I never try to act like I know more than anybody else. Being out as much as we are every single day, at least I learn a lot about my deer here in Iowa, but it might be different in other parts of the country.

"At any rate, here we are going into our eighth television season and our fourth season of *The Crush* as we approach the 2011 hunting season, and never in a million years did I think I'd

be doing this. As a kid, I'd watch the *Jackie Bushman Show* or *Realtree Outdoors*, and I'd say, 'Oh my gosh, what a dream to be able to do that,' but I never once thought I would ever be doing it myself. Since these shows came out of the South, I always thought, 'What does a kid like me from Minnesota know?'

"So I just pinch myself every day and ask myself, 'How in the world did that happen?' I guess sometimes you just get lucky. But if all of this went away today, I'd still be driving a tractor. I'd probably become a full-time farmer. But you can also bet that Tiffany and I would be out there chasing mature bucks at least 100 days a year during bow season."

CHAPTER 3

MISS CONGENIALITY:
The Girl with the Million-Dollar Smile

"Growing up, I had the greatest parents in the world and a wonderful upbringing," Tiffany said. "Even though I was pretty much a city girl, we had a cabin up north of Minneapolis, and I went fishing just about every weekend with my dad, weather permitting. I loved being with him. When I was 18, my dad died very unexpectedly of a heart attack. It was tough loss. He was a young man in his mid-40s, and he always kept himself in great physical condition. We had been very close.

"I have a wonderful mom as well. So many people I knew in high school still have both their parents, but they weren't always the greatest parents in the world. I often find myself thinking that I would gladly take the short 18 years I had with my dad any day over a long lifetime of having a deadbeat dad like so many people I've known over the years. A great dad seems to be a rare thing these days.

"Growing up, I had the greatest parents in the world," Tiffany said. Tragically, she lost her dad, Gary, to a heart attack when she was 18. "It was a tough loss. I'd give anything if he could be here now. He'd be so proud of what Lee and I have done with our lives, and he would love the fact that I've become such an outdoor girl."

We never really had a normal date. Lee would call me up and say, "Hey, you wanna go look for sheds?"

Tiffany embarked on her first bow-hunt for deer with Lee on Sept. 24, 1999. No one knew what might happen, but when the moment of truth came, she performed flawlessly, making a perfect shot on this beautiful 6-pointer. Now, more than 12 years later, she's still making flawless shots with her bow but with one big difference: The bucks she shoots now are mature giants.

"One thing really tears me up about losing my dad so early in life. Since I wasn't brought up in a hunting environment, he would have absolutely loved what I'm doing now, and he would have been so proud of me. He would have loved Lee, and I wish he could have lived long enough to see what Lee and I have done with our lives. I can just see him now. He would have been so excited.

"When I was young, I always remember my mom and dad saying, 'When we retire, we're going to do this or that.' Lee lost his mom not long after I lost my dad, and we both heard that same statement many times from our parents. 'When we retire … .' Sadly, neither my dad nor Lee's mom lived to reach retirement age. That taught us a big lesson. Because of that, Lee and I have always lived our lives a little differently. We more or less decided a long time ago that we were going to live for today.

"When we really started dating seriously, Lee was finishing college, and I was a flight attendant. We never really had a normal date. Lee would call me up and say, 'Hey, you wanna go look for sheds?'

"Of course I did. Or, he'd say, 'Let's go watch deer this evening.' I loved it. I loved being with him and doing the things we did outdoors together. I had never done any of those things, but I loved every minute of it with him.

"I remember after our fourth date or so, I asked, 'Do these things really drop their horns?' I was beginning to think this was some kind of ploy to get me out in the woods. So far, I hadn't seen a deer anywhere. But we had seen some trails, and we knew they were there.

"'Yes, they really do,' he insisted.

"My aunt and uncle from McGregor, Minn., where deer hunting is very popular, were at my mom's house one day, and they asked me, 'Where are you going?'

"'I'm going shed hunting with Lee,' I answered.

"'Yeah, right,' they said. They thought it was the funniest thing they had ever seen that their city-girl niece, who had never done anything like that before, was actually going shed hunting out in the woods. And on most of those early trips, we never did find any sheds. But that's what we wanted to do, and we had fun doing it. We were always out looking at deer, or shed hunting or doing something else pertaining to deer.

One year after taking her first buck with a bow, Tiffany arrowed her first Pope and Young buck, a beautiful Wisconsin 10-pointer scoring in the mid-130s.

"In those early days, Lee was always working at the archery shop, and I would go and hang out with him. It was always fun, because all of the people would come in and stand around, talk archery and shoot, and I thought it was really neat. Right away, Lee had me cutting and fletching arrows. After a year or two of that, he asked me one day, 'Would you like to try shooting a bow?'

"I said, 'Yeah, I'd love to try.'

"As Lee mentioned, back then there were no bows made specifically for ladies, and to get a bow down to my size was a real challenge since I had a 23-inch draw. But Lee found a PSE that he modified for me, and it worked out very well. I remember the minute I got that first bow, I was so excited. All I wanted to do was shoot, shoot, shoot. I loved it.

"While Lee was working, I would shoot on the range with all the pro shooters, and they really helped me with a lot of good advice and coaching, and I got to be a pretty good shot. Then we started going to some 3-D shoots and joined a league, and archery became a big part of our life. We belonged to an archery club that was open 24 hours. It was the coolest thing, because we had a code to get in, and since we've always been night owls, we could go over there at all hours of the night and shoot for an hour or so.

"I wish we had something like that here in Iowa, because if we did, we would certainly make use of it. But we do have a number of targets set up in our back yard, and frequently, if we happen to come home during the middle of the day for something, we often take a few minutes to shoot a few arrows.

"In those days we would literally shoot all the time, and that's what we did for fun, but we really, really enjoyed ourselves. It was sort of traumatizing for me at times, though, because whenever I shot with Lee and his buddies, he would make me shoot at the men's stakes. I'd ask him if I could shoot at the women's stakes, and he'd always say, 'No, you'll never be a better shooter unless you're shooting with us.'

"And I'd say, 'But look at my lousy score.' And he would say, 'Don't worry about your score. Just worry about your form and about shooting those longer distances.' Then he would jokingly add, 'Think about all those giant bucks you're going to shoot someday.' It did make a huge difference in my shooting. But for a while, I begged him to let me shoot at the ladies' stakes, and he would never give in.

> At first, when Lee would go on some of his longer hunting trips to Kansas during October and November, he'd say, "I'm going to be gone for three weeks," and I'd say, "Have fun, because I'm going to Maui with my mom."

Tiffany the Deer Hunter

"At first, when Lee would go on some of his longer hunting trips to Kansas during October and November, he'd say, 'I'm going to be gone for three weeks,' and I'd say, 'Have fun, because I'm going to Maui with my mom.' My mom and I would usually go to Maui on vacation every year in November because that was the month my dad had died.

"Lee and I would usually meet back after his hunting trip, or sometimes after we were back from Hawaii, I would fly down to wherever he happened to be hunting. Some of the old run-down motels he stayed in were pretty bad, and I would say, 'Good heavens. Do you expect me to stay here?' But it didn't really matter, because we were together, and we always had a great time.

Later in 2000, Tiffany shot this beautiful 10-pointer in Iowa.

"After that, I started sitting in tree stands with him more and more, and sometimes he would give me the video camera, and I would videotape any deer or other interesting things that we saw. On the days that I joined him, the weather was usually mild in the mornings — not too cold, rainy or snowy — and the afternoons were always beautiful.

"Looking back, I guess that was really best for me, because he broke me into hunting gradually, and he really did it the right way. You take somebody who has never hunted before and put them outside when it's 12 degrees and they don't see a deer all day long, and they'll start thinking, 'That was really fun,' and they can lose interest very quickly.

"So actually, he was pretty smart about the way he introduced me to deer hunting. It was all fun stuff for me, and I saw bucks chasing does and a lot of other neat things. Finally one day, he said, 'Do you want to try hunting?'

"I said, 'Gosh, I don't know if I could shoot anything.'

"'That's OK,' he said. 'If you can't, it's no big deal. But if you want to give it a try, we can go out and see what happens.'

"So we went out to a spot in Scandia just north of Minneapolis, where he had some hunting land, and I was so nervous. I didn't want to let him down, and I didn't know if I could really shoot a live deer. I remember thinking, 'I really like this guy I'm with, but what's going to happen if I can't actually shoot an animal? Will he still like me?' It also made me nervous being in a tree stand, because it's one thing to sit there with a video camera, but it's something else when you have to stand up, pull your bow back and try to make a good shot on a deer. But we had always sat in a stand together from the very beginning, and I was determined to make it work.

"Even though I was nervous, I still had that feeling of exhilaration that you always get whenever you're in a tree stand. Even now, I can't wait to get in that stand before every hunt. It's such an exciting feeling. You get up there, and all of a sudden, life just sort of shuts down. You take a deep breath and breathe in that clean air, and it somehow relaxes you. You think: 'I don't care if I shoot anything or not; it's just good to be out here.'

"Lee was behind me and slightly above me, and I was sitting with my shoulders between his legs when three yearling bucks came out. I immediately said, 'I'm going to shoot one.' It was lucky for me there were three bucks together, because during the time it took to get my release on and my bow up, the first two had already walked by. I made a good shot on the third buck at about 25 yards, and he ran a few yards out in the field and went down. I was so excited. He was a beautiful young 6-pointer, and I was thrilled.

"There was no better feeling in the world. I had no idea how much my life was about to change with the release of that arrow.

How many weddings revolve around a whitetail and bow-hunting theme? With Lee and Tiffany, it's really not surprising. They spent their honeymoon hunting in Wyoming. Then, a few weeks after they were married on Aug. 23, 2003, Lee quit his job, and the newlyweds headed to Iowa to start a new life. Little did they know that in a few years they would be America's top television hunting couple.

In 2001, her third year of hunting and first year of filming with Lee on a professional basis, Tiffany shot four nice bucks, including this 9-point heavyweight from Kansas, which scored 147 inches.

All of a sudden, my life seemed to be so much more fulfilled. I had no idea how empty my life had really been before I started hunting.

"I've heard Lee tell people that I never get buck fever or that I never get excited when I see a buck I'm going to shoot. I'm happy that he would tell people that, but he is totally wrong. I get so riled up and excited before a shot. Maybe it's a benefit that I haven't been hunting as long as he has, but I still get totally jived up. In recent years, I have gotten to the point where I get more excited after the shot, but that just comes with experience.

"Now that I've been hunting longer and longer, I'm actually worse off if I know and recognize the deer that's coming in. If it's a big buck that we've specifically targeted, I have a much harder time controlling my excitement.

"I remember one of my first good misses on film was in Kansas while I was hunting with cameraman Jason Miller. At the time, Jason hadn't seen a lot of big deer. In Iowa, we see a lot of

deer on a daily basis, and we frequently pass up certain bucks that other people would shoot. But in Kansas, you're never going to see as many deer. So when this big 162-inch 8-pointer stepped out, Jason totally freaked out.

"'Oh my gosh,' he whispered. 'That deer is a huge. You've got to take him.' I wasn't used to that, because whenever I hunt with Lee, he's always so cool and collected. 'All right, that's a nice deer,' he'll whisper. 'Get your bow, and get ready.' He's always so calm and patient. In fact, one of the bucks I shot with my bow while hunting with Lee scored 174 inches, but he was so calm that I never got excited. And I had no idea that buck was so big until after it was all over.

"But Jason was so excited that he was about to fall right out of that tree stand. It should have been the easiest shot ever on camera, but I shot right under that buck at 18 yards. Fortunately, I grabbed another arrow out of my quiver and made a second shot that went right into the boiler room.

"After the deer was down, I looked at Jason and said, 'Holy smoke. I can't believe you're having a heart attack up here in this

Tiffany is now a seasoned bow-hunter who knows her business and goes about it with great skill. This Iowa megabuck, taken in 2003, was her first real giant. The big 10-pointer grossed 173 inches.

61

In 2001, Tiffany shot this beautiful 8-pointer in Wisconsin. It appeared on the video *Whitetails, Taking it to the Extreme.*

tree stand. I'm not used to having someone falling apart in a tree stand with me, and that's probably why I missed. I'm used to someone whispering quietly, 'Here he comes. Now get you bow ready. You've got plenty of time.'

"In fairness to Jason, he was very excited, and we all get that way at times. Since that incident, he's become a very cool and collected cameraman. I guess a lot of it really is who you're with up there. If you're with someone who gets all riled up, it's pretty easy to get excited yourself. I've been really lucky to have Lee walk me through it so many times. If I have learned to stay calm, it's because of him.

"On the other hand, I'm obviously not really up on rack sizes and scores like Lee is. I know what a mature buck looks like, and I don't have a hard time passing up younger bucks. But it's nice to have someone else up there with you who knows that the buck coming in is not a shooter. It's nice to be able to analyze that buck with your cameraman to determine if he's the one you want to shoot or not. If you've got a good cameraman, you really do work together as a team.

"I don't know about most hunters, but under the right circumstances, I can talk myself into just about any deer, especially if he happens to be walking away from me when his rack looks so much wider. Several seasons back, I went 40-something days for two years in a row without shooting a deer in Iowa. After all that time and hunting every single day, every nice buck you see becomes very tempting. But you have to discipline yourself enough to hold back and make the right decision. You have to go through the mental steps that will help you do that.

"And like Lee says, when you see a buck that looks like he's going to topple over because his rack is so huge on his head, you know beyond a doubt that he's a shooter. But even when I see a buck like that, I usually have no idea what he'll score. If I ever see a 200-inch deer out there, please don't tell me, because I know I'll go to pieces.

> Every deer I have ever shot has been on video. So I never really feel any outside pressure because of the camera. I do put pressure on myself not to goof up, although it does happen a lot. And I get so upset when I miss or do something dumb.

"Every deer I have ever shot has been on video. So I never really feel any outside pressure because of the camera. I do put pressure on myself not to goof up, although it does happen a lot. And I get so upset when I miss or do something dumb. Sometimes I cry and carry on if I miss. But if you're going to hunt deer, you're going to have heartaches, and you just have to get over it and try not to make that same mistake next time. After all, it's supposed to be fun.

"I think one of the things that helped me most in my early days of hunting was the way Lee went about teaching me. He was very patient with me, and he walked me through all of my early hunts. He never got upset when I made mistakes, and we always had so much fun being together that I always wanted to keep going back. It could have been a lot different. He could have totally ruined it for me if he hadn't been like that, but thanks to his encouragement, I broke into bow-hunting for deer in a very positive way.

"After that first little buck in Minnesota, I started hunting with Lee more and more. I started going to Iowa and Kansas with him, and we did a lot of hunting on public ground. But we always found good land to hunt on. In Iowa we also knocked on a lot of doors and asked landowners and farmers if we could hunt. Some of the biggest deer we've taken to this day were shot on public ground in Kansas.

Busting Loose!

"During my second year of hunting with Lee, I hunted in Iowa, Wisconsin and Kansas. Unbelievably, I shot bucks in all three states. So I went from one small buck the first year to three the second year, two of which were really nice deer. I shot a 147-inch 8-pointer in Kansas and a beautiful 10-pointer in Wisconsin that scored in the mid-130s. A picture of me and my Wisconsin buck appeared on the cover of Gary Clancy's book, *Hunting Whitetail Deer*, published in 2000.

> Lee and I were really on a roll, and it was awesome. It wasn't that I was such a great hunter. Lee always made sure I was in a great spot, and we always hunted together.

"The year after that, in 2001, I shot four bucks. Lee and I were really on a roll, and it was awesome. It wasn't that I was such a great hunter. Lee always made sure I was in a great spot, and we always hunted together. He went to a lot of trouble to find the best places to hunt and it really paid off.

"By my fourth year of hunting (2002), we had started filming for TV so all of those hunts were recorded on video. Lee had a great season as well. In fact, he shot some of his best bucks ever that year. As soon as we started seriously filming for TV, things really worked out well for us because of our schedules. I was flexible with my airline schedule, and even with his full-time job at the refinery, Lee was able to take off a lot of time during hunting season.

"People think we had it so easy, and that our TV career just sort of fell into place as a result of being able to do what we wanted to do. But it wasn't that way at all. Everything we did revolved around our interest in deer hunting. We seldom took time off to do anything else, and any time that we had off was devoted to hunting or finding land or getting ready for the next season. We worked very hard at what we did, but we both loved doing it so much that it never really seemed like work.

"In 2003, after Lee quit his job with the refinery, we didn't have the slightest idea about what we were going to do. We were even facing foreclosure on our house in Minneapolis, but I knew how very unhappy he had been with his job. So we both said,

'Life is too short to be miserable all the time. Let's do something we really want to do.' Fortunately, we didn't have any kids, and I knew I could fly out of just about any decent-sized airport to get to Minneapolis, where I was based. So I said, 'If you want to do something different, now is the time. Let's go for it.' And we did.

"And I said, 'Thank goodness. I'd hate to think that I'd have to divorce you after only several weeks of marriage because you are such a bear that nobody could live with you and because you are so unhappy with your life. That's no way for anyone to live.

"Several years before Lee and I got married, I was working part time at Cub Foods, in the same store where my mom worked. The date was in December 1999, and I was 22 at the time. I did seasonal help during the Christmas holidays, making shrimp trays,

fruit baskets and things like that. It was hard work, but I wasn't afraid to work hard, because that's the way Lee and I were both brought up. I had just come home from a trip to Japan. At that time, I had probably been with Northwest about four or five years.

"I had flown all night long, and I was tired from the trip anyway, when my hand suddenly started to go numb. I'd been working with exotic fruits, and I didn't know if I had been bitten by something or if the fact that I had been up all night long had anything to do with it. Then my entire arm started going numb. I was a little worried, but I didn't think that it was anything really serious.

"Then a friend of my cousin's came in, and he said, 'Hey Tiffany, how's Brad? Where is he living now?' I couldn't talk. I tried to answer him and say that I had just been to Phoenix two weeks earlier to visit my cousin, but I couldn't get the words out. By then, I knew something was seriously wrong. The guy I was talking to didn't know me well enough to know that something was wrong. He probably just thought I was crazy.

"My leg started to go numb, and then the side of my face started to numb. I got really scared, and so I went to find my mom. She was working in an office that was up a long flight of stairs that was difficult to climb. The minute she saw me, she knew something was wrong. We drove to the hospital right away and discovered that I had suffered a small stroke. It took several days of testing to determine what had caused the stroke. A blood clot had developed in my lungs and gone to my brain.

"We discovered that I had been born with a hole in my heart that never closed up properly. I was told that I was going to have to have open-heart surgery to repair the hole. So I had the surgery in early January, and two weeks later, Lee and I drove to the Archery Trade Association show in Indianapolis. My mom wasn't too happy with Lee about that. 'What? You're taking Tiffany where?'

"It wasn't so bad, though. I recovered very quickly. I had to sit down and rest a lot at the show because I got tired very easily. People at the show couldn't believe it. I would tell them about the surgery, and they'd look at me and say, 'What? You just had open-heart surgery and now you're at this show? No way.'

"Lee was so supportive throughout the whole thing. He was a tremendous help during my recovery, and I was back shooting my bow within a couple of months. I was lucky that they didn't actually crack my chest open like they so often do in many open-heart-surgery procedures. They came in through my ribs instead, and that didn't really affect my ability to pull back a bow that much. Sometimes when I'm out hunting in really bad weather, my ribs will swell up and form a little knot where they were fused together, but for the most part, the surgery has never really given me much trouble."

Note: Many older men who have had open-heart bypass surgery have never been able to shoot a bow again because the surgery required that the sternum be cut open and wired back together. Although Tiffany didn't have to have that procedure, the fact that she was shooting her bow again within a short time shows just how tough and determined she really is.

That Crazy Blonde with a Bow

"After Lee left his job, I still kept my job with Northwest for two or three years, flying and doing the TV show at the same time. It worked out so well because Lee had bought his first piece of property in Kansas with friends, and he had just bought a second piece in Iowa, where we ended up living. So we owned our own property, and we were able to fly for free. We didn't have to hire a cameraman to film us because we filmed each other, and we owned our own filming equipment. So nobody was out anything.

"During those first few seasons of filming, we were able to give the video footage we shot to companies like Realtree to be used in the *Monster Bucks* series, and it didn't really cost us that much to speak of.

We were just doing it for fun, and we were having a great time doing it. It also worked out extremely well because Lee was — and is — such a perfectionist that we always had really good footage from each hunt, and people like David Blanton at Real-tree really appreciated Lee's professionalism.

"After we started our TV show *Gettin' Close*, sponsored by Scent-Lok, I think people really related to Lee and I as a couple. Instead of being an experienced outdoor woman hunter full of wisdom, I was just a ditz, and people liked that. To this day, I couldn't even tell you which direction east is standing in my own driveway. But I do have an app on my phone that will tell me. It was always more about having fun. We made fun of ourselves all the time, and I think people really liked seeing that."

Note: the dictionary definition of "ditz" is: 'A superficially dumb valley chick, with no common sense whatsoever. Usually of white race, rich and pretty." Don't be fooled. Tiffany is definitely white and pretty, and she'll tell you that she's rich in the sense of living a fulfilling life of adventure and fun with Lee, but she is anything but a dumb valley chick. When she gets out in the field with bow in hand, she is a serious, seasoned hunter who goes about her business with amazing coolness and skill.

"People started looking for that laid-back feeling in our show, but Lee and I were also shooting really good deer, and that made a big difference as well. I never shot deer that Lee wouldn't shoot. From the very beginning, Lee always said, 'You're never going to shoot a bow that I wouldn't shoot, and you're never going to shoot a buck that I wouldn't shoot.' It was very similar to our earlier days at the range, where I had to shoot on the men's level. Lee never said, 'You're a girl so you can cut corners.' Instead, we were always swinging for the bleachers, and Lee always made sure we had the best equipment and the best spots to hunt.

"We had just moved to Iowa, and we were building the house we now live in when ScentLok called Lee about doing a TV show. It was in October 2003, but Lee wasn't hunting because his 'cameraman' — me — was on a five-day trip to Japan. We were excited because Scent-Lok more or less told us we could do the show the way we wanted to do it. I had no idea what was involved with doing a TV show with all of the openers, closings and cutaways that we had to do, but I was ready to take it on and simply go with the flow.

"I remember doing our interview pieces for our first show, which happened to be a moose hunt up in Alberta. We had already been filming each other for several years, and now the main difference was that we always had several cameramen around and a lot more behind-the-scenes stuff had to be taken care of. But even back then, Lee and I still filmed each other

About the show, *Whitetail Freaks*, Tiffany said: "A lot of times when we were doing seminars at shows, or if we were traveling somewhere to hunt, people would always come up to us and say, 'If I had what you have, I could shoot big bucks just like you do.' People didn't realize how hard we worked at doing what we do. It didn't just happen.

"So Lee came up with the idea of doing a show about everyday guys shooting big deer in various parts of the country, sort of like he used to do when he first started out before he actually owned any land. These guys all had jobs, families and responsibilities, and yet they were still able to go out and shoot great deer, and *Whitetail Freaks* would show how they did it. Co-hosted by Lee and his good friend Don Kisky, *Whitetail Freaks* aired on the Men's Channel for two years. Then it moved over to Outdoor Channel, where it is today."

more than we did with other cameramen because we had to be very careful about spending money. When you do a TV show, you have to film all of your shows in one season, but you don't get paid for them until the next season, when they begin to air. So we were very cost conscious.

"*Gettin' Close* aired for four seasons on the Outdoor Channel. As it got bigger, we realized that there were numerous opportunities out there to do appearances. Also, since ScentLok owned our show, we wanted to have a little more control over our own destiny, so we decided to start a new show on Outdoor Channel in 2008.

"When we started *The Crush*, it was fairly easy for us to get sponsors because Lee had been dealing with so many people in the archery industry for so long. However, when we were first changing over to our new show, the internet had become bigger and bigger, and it was getting more and more difficult to find a name in the hunting industry that had not already been trademarked or used as a domain name. We were down in Georgia filming a commercial with Greg Ritz, our manager, and we started throwing around some potential names for the new show. Out of the blue one day, Lee said, 'How about calling our new show *The Crush*?

"We gave it some thought and realized that 'crush' could mean so many different things. It could mean that Lee and I had a crush on each other. It could mean that we have a crush or passion for whitetail hunting. Or it could mean that we were going to crush some big bucks. It was sort of off-the-wall, but everybody liked it because it seemed to fit who we were. So the name stuck. Once again, it was something in our lives that was never planned. It just kind of happened, and that's the way we've always done things.

"*The Crush* premiered on Outdoor Channel in 2008. In 2011, while we were working on this book, we were also filming for our fourth season.

Deer Shows and Other Appearances

"Although we absolutely love doing appearances and talking to people, we never planned on doing a lot of appearances at shows and sporting goods stores all over the country. But after *The Crush* got off the ground, people started asking us to do more and more seminars and autograph sessions at different shows. We realized how important it was to be out there meeting fans of the TV show. I remember a quote from Taylor Swift. She said, 'If you want a million people to buy your CDs, you have to shake a million hands.' To me, that was really great advice, and Lee and I knew that if we wanted our TV show to be successful, we'd have to do a lot of appearances.

"At first, we flew to most places, but we quickly realized how much time and expense it was taking to get to different cities. When you live in southeastern Iowa, you can't get anywhere by plane very easily. We had to commute out of Cedar Rapids, and unless we were going to Minneapolis or Chicago, we always had

As the demand increased for Lee and Tiffany to make personal appearances during the off-season, they decided to lease a bus in 2008. "It has saved us so much time and money. We love it," Tiffany said.

to change planes at least once. With travel time to the airport and layovers, it was taking us at least a full day to get somewhere and a full day to get home.

"So Lee came up with the idea of getting a bus. Several of the country singers we know — and who had started hunting with us — have their own buses for touring, and they all love them and swear by them. In our case, a bus would enable us to drive to shows or to out-of-state hunting destinations with our cameramen and crew right onboard. And by having computers and editing equipment set up on the bus, we could work all day long without any down time, sleep at night and be refreshed the next morning at a show or on a hunt somewhere. We got the bus in 2008, and right away, we started saving lots of time — and money.

"In Spring 2011, we did 14 back-to-back weekend shows and appearances traveling all over the country. We find that at every show we attend, we'll meet someone who truly touches our lives or makes a real difference in our lives. It might be a little boy or girl, or it might be an older person. Lee and I often just look at each other and shake our heads after hearing some special story. It's so easy to get caught up in your own life and get hung up on some small thing, but after hearing some of the stories we hear, it really puts our lives in perspective. That part of it has really been neat, and it doesn't just happen once in a while. It happens at just about every show or appearance we attend.

"We never planned on doing all of those appearances or selling clothing and T-shirts at shows, but people started asking us for them, so we started selling some specialty *Crush* items. We now sell DVDs of our TV shows, bracelets and necklaces, license plates, stickers, T-shirts and sweatshirts depending on the time of year. We found that there was a real market for it, and people wanted to buy our things, so we started selling them.

"How long will we keep up this hectic schedule? I suppose we'll keep doing our show as long

as people want to see it. We love to hunt, but we love to do appearances at shows during the off-season as well, and we'll keep doing both as long as we are having fun. Since we spend so much time away from home, when we finally do get home for a few days, we cherish our time there. Every day at home is a vacation to us.

"Like Lee says, 'It's a business,' and we have to run it like any other business. If you want to be successful at anything, you have to work hard at it. We never expected to be driving around in our own bus and have a line of clothing and do all of the things that we're now doing, but we really love every facet of it. Mainly, we know how fortunate we are to be living our dream."

SETTING UP THE FARM:
What to Look for When Buying or Leasing

"When Tiffany and I first moved to Iowa from Minnesota, I looked for land with lots of timber," Lee said. "I always thought, 'I need to get land with the most timber that I can possibly find.' Several of our first farms were giant pieces of timber with no open land at all. But even though I changed my thinking later on, it worked out well because most of those tracts had places where I could put in some food, and the food always brought in lots of deer.

"Many parts of the Midwest are relatively open. A lot of the land is in brush or agriculture with little wooded cover. Southeastern Iowa is blessed with a lot of wooded, rolling terrain. But I soon realized it was a mistake to concentrate on just deep woods. Sure, mature bucks spend a lot of time in wooded cover, especially during daylight when they are bedded down, but I soon realized that edge cover and open areas are equally important.

Ideally, I like tracts of 250 to 300 acres up to about 500 acres, because in Iowa — as well as many other places, but especially the Midwest — you can hold good deer on each farm with that size acreage.

Lee likes to manage properties of up to 500 or 600 acres with a mix of open land and timber.

"So I started gravitating toward land that had more of a 50-50 mix of open areas and timber. The open areas might be in CRP, old fields where cattle once grazed or just brush. I knew that some of these open areas would make great food plots. I was surprised at how many sheds we found in high grass, and I quickly learned that big bucks like to bed in grassy areas during extremely cold weather because high grass offers good cover, protection from the wind and warmth from the sun on cold winter days. High grass also provides a good hiding place. So it stands to reason that we've found a large number of big sheds in these areas through the years.

"People often ask me, 'How much land do you need to attract and keep big bucks?' Ideally, I like tracts of 250 to 300 acres up to about 500 acres, because in Iowa — as well as many other places, but especially the Midwest — you can hold good deer on each farm with that size acreage. I'd much rather have several small tracts of several hundred acres each than one large tract of several thousand acres. Even though conditions might be different on each tract, with smaller tracts, you have a lot more options available.

"Say you have a great 250-acre tract, and your food plots fail one year because of a summer drought. That could really affect your fall hunting and your ability to hold deer. But if you're managing several different tracts, you always have the option of moving over to another tract where food might not be an issue. Say you have a great piece of property, and the farmer next to you sells or leases to an outfitter. Say that outfitter allows his hunters to shoot every 3½-year-old buck they see. That could really affect your age structure and your hunting in a big way.

"By having access to several tracts, if something doesn't work out in one place, you have the option of concentrating your efforts somewhere else. A lot of things can go wrong on a larger tract of 1,000 acres or more. In truth, you can shoot a big buck on 10 acres — if it's the right 10 acres. If the 10 acres abuts a larger tract, and if conditions are right, you can do it on a consistent basis. But for my management purposes, I like to go with several hundred acres — up to 500 or 600 acres — of mixed open land and timber.

"Another good reason for having several different farms to hunt involves hunting pressure. Since I'm a fanatic about managing my land so that the deer are relatively unpressured, especially the big bucks, if you have four or five tracts to hunt on, you can spread your hunting around without putting too much pressure on one place. If you hunt just one farm, and if you're as avid a hunter as I am, you're going to want to be out there almost every day during the season. I don't care how careful you are; with that kind of centralized pressure, the deer are going to know you are hunting them.

"Say you're hunting a huge buck on a particular farm, and the wind is not right for you to hunt your stand on a certain day. If that's the only place you have to hunt, it might be tempting to go and hunt that stand anyway, or try to slip in and set up another

You can shoot mature bucks on 10-acre properties — provided they're the right 10-acre properties.

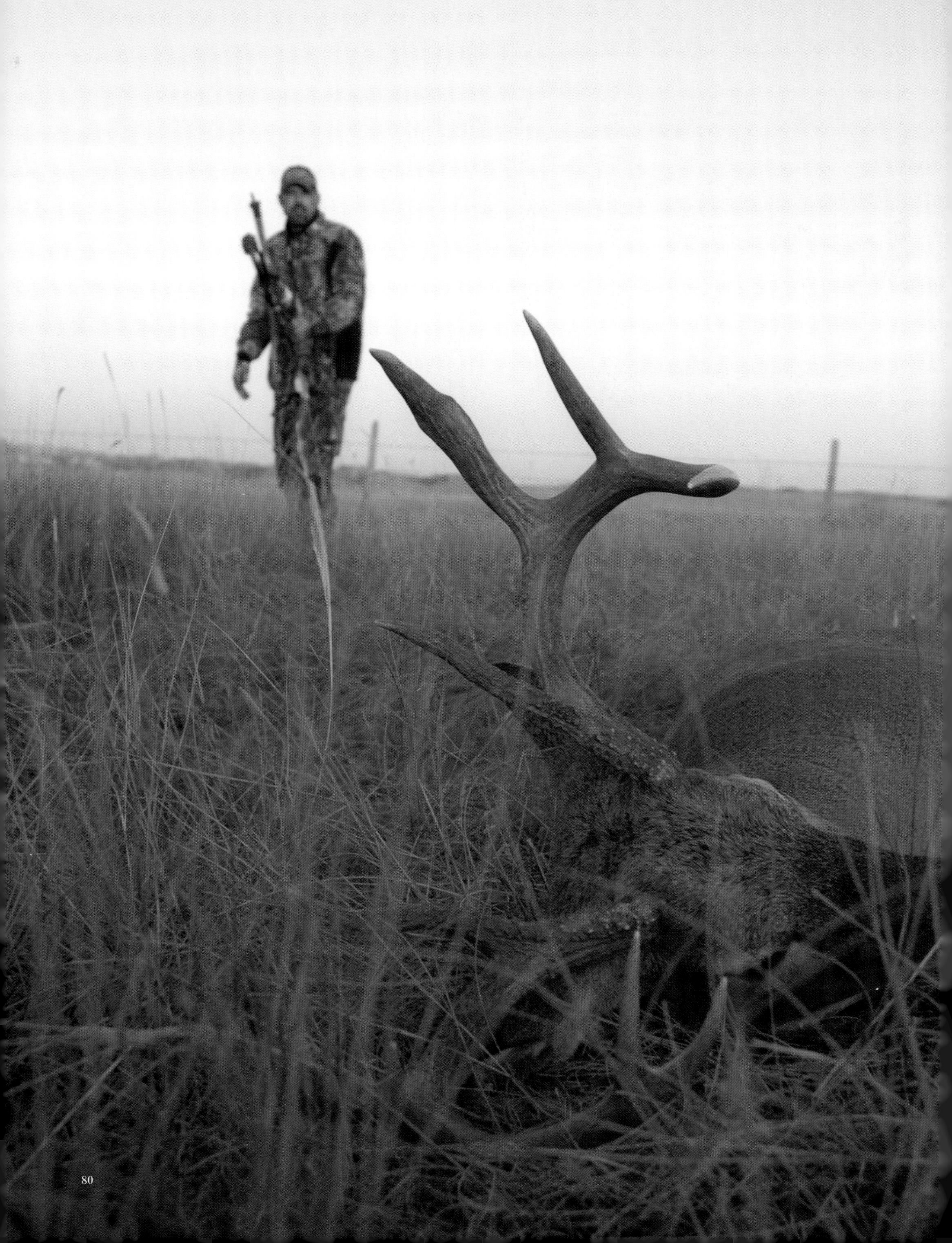

stand where the wind is right. If you do, you run the risk of running that buck out of there permanently. On the other hand, if you have another good farm to hunt, it's a lot easier letting the first place rest for a day or two and going to the other farm.

A 51-Acre Gold Mine

"I recently bought a 51-acre tract that's next to a 500-acre farm that we have because I believed the 51 acres was extremely important to the larger tract. In fact, I knew it was going to be great because the tract serves as a natural funnel that filters the deer right into our larger farm. Even though it's small in size, if that was the only piece of land I had to hunt on, I know that Tiffany and I would kill a big buck off it every year because it's the right 51 acres.

"What makes it so good? Well, there is a huge chunk of heavy timberland just to the south of it — probably 500 acres or more. Unfortunately, that land has been in a trust for a number of years, and about 20 heirs are now involved with the estate. People have inquired about trying to buy it, but because there are so many heirs involved, no one can agree on anything. So essentially, the land can't be sold right now. The owners don't hunt on the property, but they allow gun-hunters to hunt it during the shotgun season.

"The 51 acres has a lake on one side of it that serves as a huge funnel. Any deer coming from the large tract of timber to the south — and toward our food plots on the larger tract — have to funnel through one narrow portion of the 51 acres near the lake. A large cliff sits on one side of the lake, and a road is located on the other side. So the deer have to funnel through a fairly small area, especially if they want to get to the good food on the other side.

"Even before I acquired it, there were always planted farm fields on the 51 acres, so it always had some good food for the deer. Of course, since I've had it, I've converted those farm fields into great food plots. There are also crop fields on the property to the west of the 51 acres, but when those crops are harvested in fall, the only food around is on our property. And where do you think those deer are going to be when all the food in those harvested fields is gone?

"Although it's small, the 51 acres is big enough to hold plenty of deer because of the ideal food situation. And even if

Although it's small, the 51 acres is big enough to hold plenty of deer because of the ideal food situation.

Lee likes to create small access roads to stand sites so he can slip in and out of the area undetected and avoid spooking mature deer.

the deer want to go from one place to another, they have a path through the 51 acres in the form of a good funnel that will take them right onto our 500-acre tract just to the north.

"After acquiring the 51 acres, I also solved a big problem I had on the larger tract. We had seen a lot of big bucks feeding early in the morning in one of our clover fields that we call the Cabin Field, located next to the 51 acres. We were getting a lot of good trail camera photos of some of these bucks, and one in particular I had started calling Skyscraper. But all of those pictures had been taken in the morning, and there was no way to walk into that field in the morning from our side of the property without spooking every deer out there — and any that might be bedded in the edge of the woods as well. That's a common problem for hunters in many areas who want to hunt good food plots in the morning. It's so hard to get in undetected without clearing the field.

"Since there was a county road on the far side of the 51 acres, I took my Bobcat and dozed out a little woods road from that main road along one of the ridges on the 51 acres that was fairly open anyway. My road ended about 75 yards from the clover field that I wanted to hunt near the drop-off and the lake. When I had my

new road in place, if the deer were feeding in that clover field early in the morning, I could come in from my new road on my Bad Boy Buggy, sneak into my stand on the edge of the field and get set up for a morning hunt without spooking a single deer.

"A fence originally separated the two pieces of property, and the deer were always jumping the fence and coming into the clover field at one certain spot. So I cut the fence right where the deer were coming in and made a nice opening there for them to walk through without having to jump the fence. Now they're all coming through in the same spot, and I can get in there and hunt in the morning without running everything out of there. When I'm ready to leave, I can also slip right out without spooking any deer.

"People tell us all the time, 'You're lucky. You and Tiffany have a lot of good farms to hunt. I only have a 40-acre piece to hunt on,' or, 'I only have 80 acres.' Tiffany and I realize how fortunate we are to have several nice farms to hunt on in Iowa. But we also have partners on all of those farms, so each farm is hunted by a lot of people each year. However, if we only had

To shoot mature bucks, you must offer them a safe haven so they feel comfortable moving during daylight.

83

When Lee evaluates a property, he asks himself, "What have I got?" Control over the land is extremely important.

one small tract to hunt on like the 51 aces — if that's all we had — I firmly believe we would both shoot good deer off that tract every single season because it's got everything it needs to attract and hold deer.

"It wouldn't be possible to shoot five or six good bucks a year off a tract that small, but we could each shoot one good buck — I'm convinced of that. It's got lots of food, good water and good cover. The bucks that live there stay there year in and year out because they don't need to go anywhere else. So in truth, you don't have to have 500 acres or 5,000 acres. You can do just fine on 50 acres, if it's the right 50 acres. Tiffany and I realize that not everyone has the opportunity to hunt on some of the great farms that we have access to, but I'm convinced that with a little determination and hard work, any hunter in just about any location around the United States can find the same situation.

"A lot should go into making sure you get the right piece whether you buy it or lease. Whenever I'm looking at a good piece of property, if there is any open land by the road, I'll consider leasing it to a farmer as a buffer, or putting in CRP or other cover so that there is a lot of high grass, cedars or whatever that will prevent someone from seeing into the property from the road. Then I try to figure out how I can put my food plots in the middle of the property to hold the deer there as much as possible.

"I also make sure that I have good access in the form of trails or farm roads leading into those food plots that can be used during hunting season. Good food might be one of the most important ingredients in holding mature deer on your property — security is another — but being able to get in and out of your tree stand or ground blind without spooking any deer ranks right on up there in importance.

"I've actually built several small food plots in the timber around good stand locations. In those instances, I found an excellent stand site where the deer were funneling through the area for one reason or another, so I went in and dozed out a small opening right there next to my stand. And these locations have proven to be great producers.

Evaluating Hunting Land

"If I were buying a farm, I would look for good cover, enough food and a lot of edges with inside corners. Those edges are so important. But the first thing I always think about is food. I often hear people say that you can go overboard on food plots, but I don't think that's possible. I've learned that you simply can't have enough food for your deer. No matter how much food I plant each year, it's often gone by late season.

"If you've got the only food around, you'll have so many deer that come in late in the season. It's true that a lot of the deer we see are coming in from miles around, but that's fine with me because you never know when a mature 5- or 6-year-old buck that you've never seen before might decide to come in with the others. He might like what he sees and decide to stay.

"Or he might remember where that good food is and decide to come back during the rut the next year to check things out. If you think about it, when the normal farm crops come out in September and October, if you've got the only corn and beans and clover in the whole area growing on your land, where are the deer going to go?

"Whenever I look at a new piece of property, I ask myself, 'What have I got?' Control over your land is very important, and I always recommend trying to buy over leasing whenever possible. But leasing can work as well if that's your only choice — if you can get a long enough lease. If you can get, say, a five-

The Lakoskys have learned that you cannot have enough food for deer. No matter how much they plant, it's often gone by the late season.

What does the land need so that I can entice that 5½-year-old or older buck to come by my stand within bow range during daylight?

Many hunters don't realize how quickly they can turn a property around with solid management.

year lease with a five-year right to renew, you should have the time to do what you need to do and to grow some big bucks. The important thing is being able to control who goes on your land and who hunts on it.

"Since my first concern is usually food, I like to look at a piece of property and ask myself, 'Where can I tuck in one or more good foods plot well off the road so that the deer won't be bothered? Where can I put a food plot so that a 5½-year-old deer will feel safe coming out in the middle of it in broad daylight?' And more specifically, 'What does the land need so that I can entice that 5½-year-old buck or one older to come by my stand within bow range during daylight?'

"That's a pretty big order, but it can be done. To achieve that goal, you've got to be able to hold the deer on your land with good year-round food sources, and you've got to be able to offer a safe haven to those older bucks so they'll feel secure enough to want to stay on your land during hunting season. You've got to be able to protect your deer so that they can reach those older ages.

The Smith Farm Odyssey

"Some farms you look at are so good that you say, 'I've just gotta have this.' One farm that comes to mind as a great example of what can be done to a piece of property is the Smith farm, where in 2009 I shot Gnarles Barkley, one of my largest and best bucks ever. (The story about the hunt for Gnarles appears in Chapter 5.)

"Consisting of about 400 acres, the Smith farm had been for sale for several years. Although there were a lot of deer on the place, it was being hunted heavily, so the age structure was not very good. When I looked at it, I was certain there were very few — if any — 4½-year-old bucks or older on the place. Further, it had no really good year-round food sources on it. But it did have a number of hay fields that were being leased out to farmers, some of which I knew could be used for making some great food plots. And it also had plenty of water with several good creek bottoms and many acres of thick cover — mostly cedars — that the deer could use for winter cover.

"I soon found out that some of the older bucks on this property were indeed using all of that thick cover for winter habitat and protection from the cold. But I also learned that as soon as spring arrived, they moved on to someplace else because there was no food on the property to keep them there. However, those two things took a while to figure out.

"In the meantime, I asked myself, 'What would this place be like with good food on it?' Even though I knew this farm had been pounded really hard, I knew that in two years, I could increase the age structure substantially and probably have some 5½- or 6½-year-old deer on it from the 3½-year-olds that were already there.

"A lot of hunters don't realize how quickly you can turn a place around. It's amazing what a few seasons will do to the age structure of your bucks if you protect them. If you have a piece of property with some good 2½- and 3½-year-old deer, in just two short seasons you can have some great 4½- and 5½-year-olds. Then you've really got something. I also was certain that with the right kind of food, I could keep some of these older bucks on the property.

"I knew this farm had potential. And even though it had some negative issues that had to be addressed and corrected over time, I had a feeling deep inside that it could really be made into something special. As things turned out, buying the Smith farm was one of the best decisions I ever made.

"Not that I'm any smarter than the next guy. It's just that I saw the great potential this place had, and by implementing the right kinds of management strategies along with a lot of hard work, my vision for what the Smith farm was capable of producing turned out to be even better than I had ever hoped for. In truth, anyone could have done the same thing and gotten the same results."

BEST KIND OF OBSESSION:

A Buck Named "Gnarles Barkley"

"I signed the contract to buy the Smith farm in January 2007, and we had an agreement that I could go out there and shed hunt," Lee said. "I immediately put out a feeder and a couple of cameras to try to get some pictures of some of the local deer. As mentioned, the farm had lots of grown-up grassy fields that had previously been used for grazing cattle. I planned to convert most of the interior open fields into food plots. Several of them were quite large. The open land by the roads would be leased to a farmer.

"The first time I went back to look in the fields, there were already lots of deer coming to the feeder. As I was walking along the edge of the woods, I saw what appeared to be a huge antler sticking up out of the snow. I thought, 'My gosh, that looks like an elk antler.' I walked over to the spot, and there were actually two large sheds together in the snow. Because of the way the tines were sticking up out of the snow, the pair had looked like one single antler.

8/18/2009 5:20 AM

The buck named Gnarles Barkley
didn't initially stay year-round on the
Lakosky property. However, by 2009,
Lee's food plots made him a resident.

8/18/2009 5:58 AM

8/18/2009 5:40 AM

"The sheds were huge. They were fairly normal with four points to the side, but they were massive. Because of their heavy mass, I knew they were from an old, mature buck. The right antler had two stickers, and the left had one. I was pumped. I thought, 'At least there's one good deer on this place.' After I found that first set of sheds, I planted several large food plots in spring and put out several cameras. But going into summer, I never got a single picture of that special deer, and that really puzzled me. I figured he had been one of those deer that was just passing through when he dropped his antlers.

"The next winter, I found one shed antler and then the other on the same ridge where I had found the first set. I actually found the second antler less than 100 yards from where I had found the first set. 'How could that be?' I wondered. I knew immediately which deer the antlers were from. I was even more pumped and very excited.

"The second set was similar to the first, but the antlers had gotten much more gnarly. Both antlers curled up in a funky fashion at the end of the main beam, and the right antler had several stickers. I decided to call this deer Gnarles Barkley — after Charles Barkley, the 6-foot, 6-inch basketball player — because I knew the deer was huge and had a one-of-a-kind rack.

"Now I was completely puzzled. 'Is he here on the property?' I wondered. 'If not, how could a buck that's just passing through drop his antlers in almost the same place two years in a row? And if he is here, why haven't I gotten a picture of him or seen him for a whole year?'

"After that first year of not seeing him, I had been so disappointed. But now I was all excited again, and I had my hopes up. I had to believe that at the very worst, he was living on the property in the late season. Obviously, he wasn't living on the property on a year-round basis, and I knew I had to figure out a way to keep him on it. 'Maybe the heavy hunting pressure of the previous years had run him off during hunting season,' I thought.

"The property contained a lot of thick cedars and a lot of heavy timber, as mentioned. 'Maybe he's just wintering here,' I thought, 'and that's why I've found two sets of his sheds. Then, as soon as spring green-up hits, maybe he's going somewhere else.' It was a mystery, but I was determined to do everything I could to entice him stay on the property during hunting season. I believed strongly that the only way I could do that was with food. If I could give him all the food he could ever want, maybe he would decide to stay.

"By the second summer, we had corn, beans and turnips planted in our food plots, and those fields were

Gnarles had the body of an old buck. Like many older deer, he wasn't aggressive and kept his distance from younger bucks.

attracting a lot of deer. We had a lot of good 3- and 4-year-old bucks. By the third year (2009), our food plots were even better, and Gnarles had stayed. Early that summer, we started getting numerous trail camera photos of him, and we saw him several times.

"He was coming out of the same finger of woods into one of the large bean fields every evening just before dark. By watching him, I learned that he was very non-aggressive. He always kept his distance from the younger, more aggressive 3½-year-old bucks, and sometimes they sort of pushed him around through intimidation.

"I had a feeling that he might be a very old buck — possibly even 8½ or 9½ years old. He certainly had the body of an old buck, and he was huge in body size. I had noticed through numerous observations on several of our farms that a lot of old, battle-weary veteran bucks seem to lose that aggressive nature so typical of most of the younger bucks. They stay to themselves more, they're no longer interested in fighting, and they find and

Gnarles Barkley had a main-frame 4-by-4 rack with multiple stickers and abnormal points. With almost 50 inches of mass, the buck grossed 197 inches.

breed does on their own terms. They've gotten wiser through age, and they're survivors. Sometimes when you see a buck like Gnarles, it's hard to know exactly how old he is if you don't know anything about his previous history through sightings or trail-camera photos.

"He was coming out of a big patch of woods where I knew he had to be spending most of his time during the day. I knew the beans would be starting to go away in late September, and

I wondered what he would do when that happened. Would he leave again? That's when I got the idea to put in a small clover field just on the other side of the big timber where I suspected he was living. If I could get him to switch over to the clover when the beans started to die out, I knew I would have a good chance of killing him in that small field.

"I dozed out a small food plot, and I did everything I could do to make it one of the best clover fields I had ever planted. I limed the soil, I planted and fertilized, and I made sure there were no weeds growing in the clover. By late summer, it was lush, green and beautiful like I had hoped it would be. Would Gnarles take the bait? Only time would tell.

"During August, we got numerous pictures of Gnarles feeding in the beans, and I felt really good about my chances of killing him in early October as soon as bow season opened. When Tiffany and I left to go elk hunting and do some other out-of-state hunts in late August like we always do, her brother Jason checked the cameras on a regular basis for us. As usual, we were gone for the entire month of September. During that time, the cameras failed to record a single picture of Gnarles. As each day in September drifted by, I got more worried that he might be gone.

"Was he still around? No one could say for sure, but by now, something else had happened. I was totally obsessed with this deer. During the entire time we were gone, I thought about him day and night. I daydreamed about getting home so I could hunt him.

> During August, we got numerous pictures of Gnarles feeding in the beans, and I felt really good about my chances of killing him in early October as soon as bow season opened.

A Hope and A Prayer

"If Gnarles hadn't already left the property in late August, there was another worry. As soon as all of the other more aggressive bucks started peeling out of velvet around the first of September, they might run him off. That's the time when they all start getting a lot more aggressive and start pushing each other around. I hoped that he hadn't left the property and that he was going to that clover field, but I was worried sick that he had been pushed off the property. By this time, there were so many other bucks out there. I thought, 'Man, as non-aggressive as he is, those other bucks might make him leave the property and go somewhere else.'

"We had been away hunting for most of September, and we didn't get home until late in the afternoon on Oct. 3. While driving home that day, all I could think about was Gnarles. I wanted

to find out what was going on with him in the worst way, but it was much too late in the afternoon to go hunting when our bus finally pulled into the driveway. I knew there were probably deer already feeding out in the clover field, and I wanted badly to go sit in my ground blind that I had set up weeks earlier. But I knew if I did, I would probably blow all the deer out of there.

"So I said to Tiffany, 'Let's just drive over there, walk down the trail and see what's in there.' I knew with the S-curves I had intentionally built into the trail leading into the field, we could sneak right up to the edge of the clover without being seen by any feeding deer. And that's what we did.

"Well, wouldn't you know it? We got to the edge of the field, peeked around the corner, and there was only one deer feeding in that clover — Gnarles. And it was still early for a buck like him — only 6 o'clock. In that instant, I knew that all of my worrying, all of my planning and scheming, and all of the work I had put into the clover field was going to pay off.

"But at the same time, I was kicking myself and saying, 'Gosh, why didn't we get home an hour earlier? I would have been right here in my ground blind.' Deep down inside, I was really glad to see him and so relieved to know that he had not left the property.

> **Because Gnarles had me so excited, there were no other deer that I was the least bit interested in shooting at any of our other farms.**

"The next day, I didn't even hunt in the morning. Because Gnarles had me so excited, there were no other deer that I was the least bit interested in shooting at any of our other farms. We decided to wait until afternoon, because we figured that would be our best chance to see him again. Since Tiffany and I had been gone for a full month, my regular cameraman, George Novosel, had earned some time off, and he had gone home to see his wife and kids for a few days. So Tiffany went with me that afternoon to run the camera.

"After we got in the ground blind and had been sitting there a while, Gnarles came out on the northern side of the field to our right. He walked out into the clover a few feet and just stood there staring at the blind. He didn't move a muscle for a full 10 minutes. He was way over to our right, and Tiffany was leaning forward and trying to film him, and I said, 'No, no, no, don't even move.'

"I didn't want her to breathe. I didn't want either of us to breathe, but she did end up getting a little bit of footage. By that time, he was probably only 30 yards away. If we hadn't been trying to film the hunt, and if there hadn't been a camera next to me, I probably could have moved over in the blind and made a shot, but because of the camera, there was no way I could get a shot at that angle.

"So we just waited. He continued to stare at the blind. Every once in a while, he would put his head down and take a quick bite, but he kept looking toward us suspiciously the entire time. Finally, he just turned around and walked back into the woods. I was so disappointed. I knew I had him right there, but you can see in the footage Tiffany shot out of the corner of the blind that he was staring at it, and there was something about it he didn't like.

"The mesh in the windows had been down all summer long, and we had the mesh pulled up so that we could film through the open windows. That's the one downside of filming out of a ground blind, and I'm sure those open windows must have looked different to Gnarles. He hadn't been super spooked or anything like that, and he was still feeding before he walked back into the woods, but he had been very nervous just the same.

"The next day, Tiffany and I went back to the ground blind at about the same time, and two young bucks came out fairly late in the afternoon. We had named one of them Skyscraper. He was a promising 2½-year-old at the time. We called the buck with him Gnarles Jr. Junior was a 3½-year-old that was the spitting image of Gnarles Sr., only much smaller. (He never showed up the next year, when he would have been 4½, and we suspected that he had died. Or he could have been run off the property by other bucks, because at the time, there were a lot of extremely aggressive bucks on that farm.) Skyscraper and Gnarles Jr. were joined by a couple of does that afternoon, but Gnarles Sr. never made an appearance.

"On the third day, there was an east wind, and we couldn't hunt the ground blind. Our good friend Gary LeVox, of Rascal Flatts fame, was hunting with us, and we took him over to another farm where we'd been hunting a big buck named Caribou. We set up a tree stand that day where you could hunt with an east wind, and that evening, Gary shot Caribou from his stand. I didn't even hunt that afternoon. Instead, I just watched a field for Tiffany, looking out for a buck that she was after. We were all happy that Gary had shot a good buck.

"In the meantime, George had come back from his short trip home. The next day, Oct. 7, we had the west wind that I needed, so George and I went out to the clover field. We trimmed a few limbs near the blind on the northern edge because that was

The hunt for Gnarles Barkley taught Lee several lessons, including the importance of having a food plot in a specific spot.

where Tiffany and I had seen Gnarles two days earlier, and that was where we expected him to come out again.

"After a while, a nice 3½-year-old buck came out into the clover and started making a scrape and rubbing his antlers in some limbs on the edge of the field across from us. He was accompanied by a yearling spike.

"All of a sudden, both of their heads popped up and looked to the southern side of the field. George and I knew something was there. We looked over, and Gnarles stepped out of the woods on the opposite side of the field. Wouldn't you know it? We were all set up to shoot to the right because that's where Tiffany and I had seen him, and he came out on our left side. I said, 'Oh my God.'

"The 3½-year-old buck immediately bristled up and started walking toward him. Gnarles was about 70 yards away, and he just stood there like a statue staring at those two bucks. But when that 3½-year-old got close to him — all bristled up with his ears laid back — Gnarles ran out into the middle of the field. Now he was only 60 yards away. He eventually put his head down and started feeding, quartering toward us. The other buck never came close to him, although he moved toward Gnarles at one point, and Gnarles sort of tucked his head and moved away from him.

"Amazingly, Gnarles never even looked at the ground blind like he had done two days before — not one time. He kept slowly quartering toward us, and I decided to wait for the perfect shot. Finally, he turned broadside at 52 yards, and it was time to go into action. From where we were sitting, there was a slight rise in the clover field between the ground blind and Gnarles. So I came to full draw and aimed low for his heart.

"By aiming low at that distance, if he crouched down or tried to jump the string, I figured my shot would still be good. And it was. He ran into the woods and went down just inside the tree line. What a hunt. I was pumped. So many things had come together to make that moment a reality, and I had just taken one of my best bucks ever.

"He was old; I could tell that. He had that huge cinder-block body, and he easily could have been 8½, 9½ or even 10½ years old. He had a main-frame 4-by-4 rack with several stickers and abnormal points. He had a 10-inch brow tine on his right side and four stickers. He had multiple burr points on his left side, and the main beam curled up and back in a strange fashion, just like his shed from the year before had done. With almost 50 inches of mass, he grossed 197 inches.

> He was old; I could tell that. He had that huge cinder-block body, and he easily could have been 8½, 9½ or even 10½ years old.

Conclusion

"The hunt for Gnarles Barkley taught me several important things. I had put in that food plot in that particular spot just for him, and my strategy had worked perfectly. If you've got big deer feeding out on a bean field during early season, you've got to realize that as the hunting season progresses, those beans will start to die back and lose their protein and palatability. When that happens, the deer are going to move off of that field to another food source.

"Of course, those big bucks are also changing their patterns and going from their summer bachelor groups into a more solitary lifestyle as the pre-rut begins to kick in from the first of September to the first of October. So you've got to figure out where they're going next.

"And if you've got that desirable food available on your land like Buck Forage Oats, clover, wheat or something growing at that time of year that they want and like, there's a good chance you'll find them in that midseason food source. I've learned that

Lee admits that he was hopelessly obsessed with putting an arrow in Gnarles Barkley. Ultimately, his strategy succeeded.

if you have bean fields loaded with good bucks in early season, you'd better have something green growing that's ready for them to move onto when those beans start dying down.

"Gnarles was so docile at his advanced age that I knew I wouldn't be able to rattle him in. I knew from experience that if I tried to rattle in a buck like him, he'd just go the other way. Old bucks like him simply don't do much fighting. They leave it to the younger bucks. We've found that to be the case with so many of our older bucks.

"Gnarles was one of those bucks that a hunter can easily become obsessed about. I had found his sheds for two years in a row. But I had never seen him during hunting season or gotten a picture of him until that second year, and there's no question that I was hopelessly obsessed with putting an arrow in him. When you're obsessed, after not seeing a buck for so long, you begin wondering, 'What the heck is going on?'

In Gnarles' case, I knew he was wintering on the farm where I shot him, because I had found his sheds for the past two years in a row. But he wasn't staying there during summer or, up until the time I killed him, during hunting season, because I never saw him or got any trail camera pictures of him during the season. And I kept cameras out all the time. If he had been there, I would have gotten his picture. Where he was going I don't know. I do know that the food I planted just for him had to be the main reason he was still there in October the year I finally killed him.

"By putting in that small food plot, I had a place that was easier to hunt than the much larger bean field where I'd always seen most of the other bucks on the property. What's more, up until that time, the new field had never yet been hunted. It had never had a stand or camera in it until I put up that ground blind, and it was the ideal situation for an old buck like Gnarles. Would he take the bait? As things turned out, he did, and I ended up having one of the greatest hunting experiences of my life.

"I saved tooth samples from Gnarles' jawbone and plan to have them analyzed for an exact age, but so far, I haven't gotten around to it."

CHAPTER 6

PLANTING AND MAINTAINING FOOD PLOTS

There's an old saying in real estate about what makes a piece of property really valuable: location, location, location. According to the Lakosky doctrine, the thing that makes a farm valuable for deer hunting is food, food and more food. Next to the food factor comes protection and low hunting pressure. Lee's philosophy is simple. If you can offer your mature bucks plenty of good food on a year-round basis and a sense of security so those deer feel safe on your land, your chances of keeping them on your property increase dramatically.

Because food is one of the most important components of Lee's total hunting program, to say that he is a perfectionist about his food plots would be an understatement. In truth, Lee is a farmer at heart. He loves being behind the wheel of a tractor, and he does most of the disking, planting and fertilizing of his food plots himself. Because he has so many

Lee and Tiffany know that offering bucks great year-round food sources keeps deer on their property year-round.

food plots to plant, this is a huge annual undertaking. Amazingly, he never drove a tractor until he and Tiffany moved to Iowa about eight years ago. But now, when you see him behind the wheel of a huge John Deere, he looks like he was born to handle just about any type of farm equipment.

"He's a fanatic about making sure the soil is turned over just right and making sure that all of his rows are perfectly lined up," said Linda Profant, Tiffany's mom. A city girl like her daughter, Linda moved to Iowa from the Minneapolis area several years ago to be closer to Lee and Tiffany, and she loves her new life on the farm. And just like her daughter, she can often be found

10/18/07   6:39 PM

in the fields, helping out in various ways during planting season. It's not unusual to see her on the back of a planter with Tiffany, making sure that the seed is being dispersed evenly while Lee drives the tractor.

"I kid Lee all the time about what a perfectionist he is," Linda said with a smile. "He is never satisfied unless all of his rows are lined up perfectly, and I tell him the deer don't care. They'll still eat the corn and soybeans even if some of those rows are a little crooked."

Lee might be a fanatic about what he does, but the hard work and sweat equity that he puts into his hunting land is enormous. However, it clearly pays big dividends. Without question, it's a labor of love, but his work ethic and energy level might be characterized as being almost super-human. The man is driven, and it's not in his makeup to do things half-heartedly or in sloppy fashion.

After all, the ultimate prize in his eyes is a mature white-tailed buck that's 5 or 6 years old, and the older bucks that he and Tiffany set their sights on don't come easy. So in spring, when those

Lee and Tiffany's small food plots are their killing plots. They plant them specifically to hunt, and they're almost always on the interior of the property.

long, green rows of young corn stalks or soybean shoots start popping out of the ground like little soldiers standing at attention, you can see the pride beaming in his face. Fanatic or not, there is always a lot of satisfaction in a job well done.

Through the years, Lee has fine-tuned his food-plot program at the farms he hunts by experimenting with various deer foods. His extensive experience and knowledge make it almost easy for him to know exactly what he needs to do on every food plot each season — and how to do it. Each farm has its own set of challenges and obstacles to overcome, and Lee is always thinking outside the bubble; planning, scheming and trying to improve and fine-tune his already highly advanced food-plot program.

"We basically have two kinds of food plots on most of our farms," Lee said. "I plant large food plots on all of the farms we hunt to help hold the deer on those farms and help carry the deer through winter. Our larger plots might range in size from 10 to 25 acres. We also plant dozens of small food plots that might range anywhere from one-half acre to an acre or two. Some-times, I'll doze out a good spot in the timber, or I'll use a small field or opening in the woods that was already there.

"These small food plots are our killing plots, and I put them in specifically to hunt over. You'll almost always find them in the interior of the property, well away from any roads. Before I ever put in a food plot, I always make sure that I have a good idea of how I'm going to hunt it and where I'm going to place my stands. I also make sure that I have a good way of getting in and out of those stands without spooking deer, for morning hunts and afternoon hunts.

"I plant corn and soybeans on most of my larger plots. I usually plant about half and half — that is, 50 percent corn and 50 percent soy-beans. I rotate the locations of these two crops back and forth each year because the beans put nitrogen back into soil while corn takes it out, and I always want to keep the soil as healthy and as nutrient-rich as possible.

> On every farm we hunt, I try to make sure the deer have good food sources for every month of the year, especially in late winter, when it's cold.

"As I've stated over and over again, you can't have too much food. On every farm we hunt, I try to make sure the deer have good food sources for every month of the year, es-pecially in late winter, when it's cold. Because most of my larger food plots butt up against mature timber, I'll often plant clover around the edges of the timber for a distance of about 20 yards all the way around the food plot.

"I've found that if you try to plant corn right next to big timber, the trees suck all of the nutrients out of the soil, and the corn is not going to do well. The stalks might not even produce a single ear of corn. So I plant clover instead. It does extremely well, and the deer love it. They love to ease out of the woods late in the afternoon and start feeding on the lush clover. Then they like to work their way out into the corn and soybeans.

"Normally, I don't plant corn or beans on any of my smaller plots. If you have a lot of deer on your property, as we do, they'll wipe out the plants on a 2-acre field or a one-half-acre field before they ever put a bean on them. My smaller plots are planted in clover, wheat, Buck Forage Oats, turnips or something similar that's green, fresh and palatable.

"That way, the deer always have a high-protein food source during hunting season. Through the years, I've experimented with just about every type of seed available for food plots, and I use many different types of seed each season. I'll try anything new that comes out on the market, and if it works well for me, I'll continue using it.

Lee keeps a detailed planting book to keep track of his exhaustive management efforts.

"I keep a planting book in my tractor, and in that book I record the date, temperature, soil conditions and the amount and type of fertilizer used in every food plot I plant. At the end of the season, I look in that book and ask questions like, "What kind of crop did I get?' 'What did I do wrong?' 'Did I plant too early or too late?' and 'What do I need to do differently?' I look at every field and make adjustments accordingly for the next season. It's amazing how much I learn every year.

The Magic of Clover

"People ask me all the time, 'If you could put in one all-around plant that would be a magic bean for your deer, what would it be? My answer is clover. Clover has about 30 percent protein, it withstands heavy grazing, it grows well in dry weather, and it doesn't die out like alfalfa. It's good for antler growth during summer, it stays green throughout winter, and the deer just love it. And the first thing that really starts growing again in early spring is clover. The deer and turkeys are all over it in late winter or early spring. For that reason, we find a lot of sheds in our clover.

"But you have to make sure that you don't plant one type of clover alone. It's important to get a whitetail blend that contains several different varieties. If you were to plant white clover by itself, for instance, it loses its palatability and protein when it gets mature, and it gets stemmy. Eventually, you have to mow it back down again.

"But if you plant a blend of whitetail varieties, the various plants grow at different rates and mature at different times, so that when one is maturing, the next one is prime. When that one gets mature, the next one is prime, and so on. With several varieties, you can also go a much longer period of time without mowing and keep a palatable clover in that field for longer.

"So if I could plant one thing, it would be clover for those reasons. Most of our hunting in early season is done over clover fields, and early season is the time when we shoot most of our biggest bucks. Clover is always a mainstay for us. In our small food plots — which are an acre or two, or even as small as one-half acre or one-quarter acre — we usually put in clover, or a turnip and rape mixture. That's because when they get on that

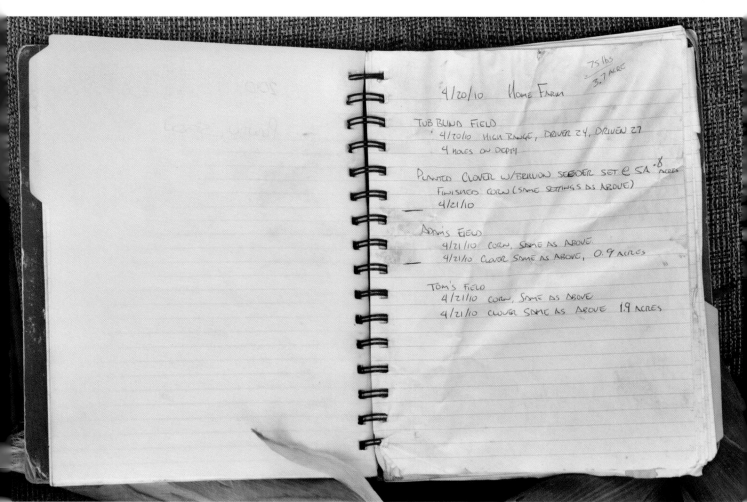

mixture, they'll wipe it out pretty fast. But the nice thing about turnips and rape is that the deer really don't touch them until later in the season after you've had a hard frost.

"And a lot of times, on a new farm where the deer have never had food plots and never tasted turnips or rape, they won't eat it at all or even touch it until January, when nothing else is left. Then they'll go eat it and realize they like it, and they'll be all over it. After that, they'll remember it the next year, and they'll be in there eating it again right after the first big freeze. All of those starches in turnips and rape are not very palatable until the plants freeze, causing those starches to turn into sugar, and then the deer eat them like crazy.

"On my small food plots, you can plant turnips and let them get to the sizes of small baseballs. The deer won't touch them or the big leafy rape plants until cold weather. During hunting season around November, I've had really good luck during the rut hunting some of my smaller fields, because the deer will be in there all over those plants. And even though they'll often wipe it all out within a couple of weeks, the timing is perfect because it happens during hunting season.

"Further, if you've got some big, baseball-sized turnips that are frozen in the ground, they'll eat the tops off them pretty fast. But it'll take them a while to dig out the bulk of the turnips that are frozen down in the ground. They might keep working on them for a month or longer so they actually last quite a bit longer than you might think in a small field.

"Antler King has a product called Fall/Winter/Spring Food Plot Blend that I like very much. Basically it's a mixture of winter rye, winter wheat and winter peas. It stays green all winter long. In spring, it's the first thing to green up along with our clover. So the turkeys and deer are all over it right away.

> Our strategy for the early season is simple. In the mornings, we try to sneak into the smaller food plots in the timber and get set up in our stands without disturbing the area.

The Killing Fields

"Normally, the smaller plots that we call our killing fields are very secluded by design, and they're the ones we really try to focus on for hunting during early bow season. They're always tucked into the timber somewhere, never close to any roads and never within sight of any road. Even if they're bigger fields (1½ to 2 acres), they have to have good pinch points or something else that makes them attractive to deer. A lot of times, I'll leave small islands in the larger fields so the deer have a lot of cover and feel safe about stepping out into the open. Basically all of our smaller food plots are set up for bow-hunting, although we

Planting and maintaining numerous food plots is a full-time job for Lee and Tiffany.

do sometimes hunt them during late muzzleloader season.

"You hope that the deer are feeding in the larger fields at night, especially just before daylight. So our strategy for early season is simple. In the mornings, we try to sneak into the smaller food plots in the timber and get set up in our stands without disturbing the area. Then, as the deer are coming off the larger fields and moving toward their bedding areas, they'll often hit those secluded fields in the timber because they feel safe and secure in those fields, and we might get a chance to see them during daylight hours. That's where we often shoot some of our best bucks during archery season.

"Of course, our mainstay in those smaller fields at that time of year is always clover. But sometimes, we'll put in some Buck Forage Oats or winter wheat. We'll plant it in late August or early September so that when everything else is dying back in October and November, that's the one thing that will still be growing. And just as I do with clover, I mow it back when it gets long, and it'll start growing again. The oats and wheat will withstand quite a bit of grazing, but nothing withstands heavy grazing as well as clover.

"Even though our larger food plots are planted primarily in corn for feeding the deer over winter (the beans are long gone by then), we do sometimes hunt those larger fields during bow season as well. We have to use a little different strategy on the larger food plots, such as relying on decoys, rattling or calling. We also put out rubbing posts in critical places near the edges of these larger fields where we have stands." (For more about rubbing posts, see Chapter 9.)"

For Lee, planting and maintaining so many food plots is really a full-time job. Getting everything together is like assembling the pieces of a big never-ending puzzle. It takes a lot of time, money and equipment, including tractors, planters, tillers, lime, fertilizer and seed. From spring through late summer, planting never really stops. And at $4 per gallon for diesel fuel, Lee went through about 70 gallons a day during the 2011 spring planting season.

"In an ideal year, I'll plant corn, beans and clover in June, and rape and turnips in July. After that, I start working on fall clover, Buck Forage Oats and wheat by the last week in August or early September. But the last few seasons (up until Summer 2011), we've had unusually heavy rains that have really put things behind. It's always something. A few years ago, we had a drought in early and midsummer, and much of my corn and beans on several farms never made it. So much depends on weather.

"My goal is to have enough food planted on each farm to last through April (spring green-up). But no matter how much I plant, I usually can't get it to last much past February. I keep very precise records on each food plot on each farm — the results of any soil tests, how much lime and fertilizer were needed, what I planted each year, and how the plots did. I've used just about every food plot product and seed on the market, and I've learned through trial and error what works and what doesn't work. If something doesn't work, or if the deer don't like it, I'll use something else next time.

"In areas where the clover grows thick, I mow it and bale it in late summer, and I feed the bales in late winter when food is scarce, just like feeding hay to cattle. In a good year with adequate rain, I can often get three cuttings of clover during the summer months, and it's still very nutritious. Baled clover is invaluable in late winter when there's a lot of snow on the ground. It's a great supplement at the time of year when the deer need it the most.

"Our clover fields are really important to us. They're like protein pellets for the deer in March and April. Clover is our magic bean. It provides 30 percent protein in the summer. It doesn't die out, and the deer always love it as long as you plant different varieties.

> I've used just about every food plot product and seed on the market, and I've learned through trial and error what works and what doesn't work. If something doesn't work, or if the deer don't like it, I'll use something else next time.

Remember Those Food Plots in the Late Season

"Most hunters think about planting in spring and late summer. But by the time deer season is finished in late January, a lot of people are over hunting for the year and thinking about ice-fishing, skiing or turkey season in spring. They're thinking about everything except the condition of their food plots.

"I have a favorite saying: The last day of one hunting season is the first day of the next. I believe all serious whitetail hunters should have that mindset. For us, the end of hunting season is a time when we really focus in on our food plots, and we immedi-

ately start thinking about the next season. We evaluate what we've done and how well certain food products worked, and we start planning for the spring planting season.

"Obviously, there's nothing you can plant in late winter, but you should be thinking ahead about what you might need to plant in the spring for next season's food supply. You should be asking yourself questions like, 'What worked, and what

For us, the end of hunting season is a time when we really focus in on our food plots, and we immediately start thinking about the next season.

Intensive management will improve a property every year as more deer start using food plots.

didn't?' and 'Were my corn fields, bean fields and turnip plots large enough to carry the deer through the entire season?'

"A lot of factors can affect how well our food plots turn out. If there isn't enough food to last until spring green-up, we sometimes resort to using feeders in late season. We feed a combination of corn and high-protein pellets. In lean years, this helps get the deer through the coldest part of the winter.

"So many times in January, February and March, mature bucks will start to show up on certain farms where we've never seen them before. In a lot of cases, this happens because we're the only show in town. That is, we've got the only food around.

If you can hold these bucks over the winter, and if they get in the habit of coming into your food plots on a regular basis, there's a good chance you can keep them on your property throughout spring when you start planting new food plots. After that, they might become permanent residents and stay through hunting season. That's what you want. And it's so easy to accomplish with good food.

Give Your Food Plots Time to Produce

"Sometimes it takes a year or two to condition your deer to new food plots, so don't get discouraged if the deer don't use them as heavily as you'd like the first year, especially with cold-weather foods like rape and turnips. Deer are creatures of habit, and it might take them several years to get in the habit of visiting certain food plots on a regular basis.

"I've had a number of instances on several of our farms where I've gone in and planted maybe 10 or 20 acres of corn for late season, and the deer only ate about one-third of it the first year. After seeing the lack of interest, I was even tempted to plant something else. But as time went on and as I continued to plant those same plots each year, the deer started mowing them down like there was no tomorrow. It just took a while.

"I remember planting about 20 acres in corn and beans on one of the first farms we ever had in Iowa. That first year, at least 18 acres of it was never touched. Now, some nine years later, you'll commonly see 200 deer out in that same 20-acre field, and the food is usually completely gone by the end of hunting season. So no matter what you plant — corn, beans, clover or turnips — don't get discouraged if the deer don't wipe it out that first year. Every year it should get better, and you should start to see more and more deer in those food plots."

11/22/08 5:52 PM

Popular misconception: Lee and Tiffany shoot a lot of big bucks because they live in an area spilling over with huge deer. True, they live in one of the country's prime big-buck strongholds, but they spend 365 days a year planning, working hard and planting to produce an environment where big bucks can be hunted successfully. First and foremost, that includes giving the local deer the nutrition they need to grow big antlers and healthy bodies. Second, it includes giving the deer the protection needed to achieve older age classes. And last, it includes providing an environment where deer feel safe and secure so they'll stay on the farms. Low hunting pressure is critical toward achieving this goal.

SUPPLEMENTAL FEEDING AND OTHER MANAGEMENT STRATEGIES

"We do some amount of supplemental feeding at different times of the year on some of the farms we hunt, often out of necessity," Lee said. "For example, we've hunted a few farms that were mostly covered in timber when we first got them. Because they were so heavily wooded, all we could initially do on these farms was put in a few small food plots in the woods that were used primarily to hunt over. Obviously, you're not going to feed deer all winter long on small food plots. So until we could doze in a couple of larger winter food plots or acquire adjacent land for some much bigger plots, we put out feeders on those places to help get the deer through the winter.

Lee and Tiffany feed a mixture of corn and high-protein pellets. Baiting is not legal in Iowa, so they never feed deer during the season.

"We feed a mixture of high-protein pellets and corn. Because baiting is not legal in Iowa, we never feed during hunting season. Even if baiting were legal, I would much rather put in a 20-acre cornfield than go in every two weeks to fill the feeders. When the corn crop is in, you're done with it. But if you're feeding pellets or bagged corn, you constantly have to go in to fill the feeders and fix broken timers. It's a lot of work, not to mention the fact that I don't like driving into the property and disturbing the deer.

"I wish all of our food plots would last through winter until spring green-up, but they don't. So much of our feeding is done in late winter, when the deer need high protein the most. But I also like to put out corn in late summer (late July and August), as soon as the deer have pretty much reached full antler growth, to get trail photos.

"Late summer is the time when you really want to see those deer, because they've reached full antler growth and you want to see how big they are, and you want to be able to study their racks. In some cases, cameras placed near feeders on the edges of fields can tell you which trails the deer are using as they come out of the woods to feed. This information can be invaluable in planning your hunting strategy a month or two later.

"People often say, 'Hey, I live in the Corn Belt in Kansas, Iowa or Illinois, and the deer always have plenty of food everywhere because of all the corn and other agricultural crops available, so I don't really need to supplemental feed or plant any food plots. My deer already have big bodies and big racks.' My response is always the same: Except in a few isolated situations, just about all of the corn and other crops that were planted by farmers in those areas will be gone by late winter, when the deer need it the most.

"When a deer goes into spring in great shape, carrying a little extra fat with his body weight up, then he puts everything he eats from that time forward into his antler growth. So the chances are good that he'll grow a great set of antlers — at least what he's capable of. But if you don't have any winter food available during the coldest and harshest winter months in December, January and February, when the deer need it the most, it's a different story.

"Yes, they might survive the winter, but even with big-bodied deer that have great genetics, they're going to have a lot of catching up to do, and a lot of those nutrients taken in spring will be going back into trying to build up their bodies first. So they're already going to be behind with their antler growth.

"I'd be willing to bet that with good year-round nutrition, you can put on 20 to 30 antler inches with some of your top-end deer just by making sure that those deer go into the antler-growing season in great shape with their body fat levels where they should be. And yes, that includes big-bodied Midwestern deer that live in the Corn Belt.

"You can take almost any mature deer with a big body and great genetics, but after he goes through the rut and gets all beat up, and after he's subjected to a cold, harsh winter with little food and a prolonged

Late summer is an ideal time to put out corn. Bucks have reached their full antler growth, and feeding lets you get numerous trail-camera photos.

Deer cross creeks and sloughs all the time, but they seldom stop to drink. Lee believes that's because they don't want to expose themselves. He builds small watering holes near bedding areas.

cold spell with below-zero temperatures for days on end, he'll end up in the worst shape of his life, with little or no body fat. He might not even survive the winter. Plenty of bucks die at this time of year because they are not in shape to survive a harsh winter.

"On the other hand, the deer that stay on our farms always go into the antler-growing season in great shape because we're going to have alfalfa, wheat, beans, clover (baled clover), corn and other grains available to them, and that also gives them a lot of incentive to stay on our farms in relative safety without having to go and search for winter foods in other areas.

Soil Tests

"Whenever we get a new farm to hunt on, or if I decide to put in a new food plot somewhere, I always take soil samples to find out what kind of soil we have and to make sure the pH is correct — especially if it's in the timber. In fact, I'll take samples for the first two or three years in row until I know the soil is right. But after we get the soil limed properly and a good pH reading of around 7, I don't usually continue taking soil samples every year unless there is an apparent problem somewhere.

"Because a lot of my small plots are in the timber, where the soil is very acidic because of the abundance of oak and other hardwood trees, and all the hardwood leaves that fall, it usually takes a lot of lime to neutralize that soil and get things right so that my clover, oats or whatever we plant will grow well. If you've got a low pH of, say, 4.5 or 5 in those timber fields, you can put all the fertilizer you want on your plants, but it won't do you a bit of good if the soil is too acidic. You'll just be wasting your money, and those plants will never grow well.

Because the correct pH gives the plants the ability to absorb nutrients out of the soil, if you have a low pH, it'll take a lot of lime to get the acidity out of the soil. Sometimes, we'll put out up to 200 tons of lime per year on all of our various food plots, with about 2 to 3 tons per acre going into our timber fields. And on a new food plot, you normally won't see the results of that lime until the second or third year. If you put out rock lime and disk it in, it takes about two years to start seeing some positive results.

The deer that stay on our farms always go into the antler-growing season in great shape because we're going to have alfalfa, wheat, beans, clover (baled clover), corn and other grains available to them, and that also gives them a lot of incentive to stay on our farms in relative safety.

So the first year, I usually put out pelletized lime along with the rock lime because the pellets absorb into the soil at a faster rate, although they're only good for that first year.

"When you get your soil up to a pH of about 7, it should be about right for enhancing plant growth. But on a new farm, it's been my experience that it might take up to three years to get it to that point, as mentioned. After that, it's just a matter of applying the right amount of fertilizer on your fields each year for maximum output. Your local ag center ought to be able to tell you exactly how much fertilizer you need to put out based on your previous year's yield. For instance, they'll ask you, 'What kind of corn crop did you get?'

"If your answer is 150 bushels per acre, they'll know exactly how much nitrogen and how much potash was removed from the soil, and how much fertilizer you need to put out to replace it. When you have your soil where you want it, your planting program becomes a yearly maintenance program, and you don't have to take soil samples every year. But even then, I'll usually take some soil samples about every third year just to make sure some nutrient isn't lacking and that things are where I want them to be.

Mineral Stations

"I like to put mineral stations out in the edges of fields containing large food plots. Certainly, minerals are an important part of our overall nutritional program, but I use them mainly to concentrate the deer in a small area to try and get pictures. I'll always have a camera set up next to a mineral station, and we have as many as 10 mineral stations on some farms.

"Because I have to go in and refresh the minerals every few months, I try to put the stations in places where I can get to them fairly easily without alarming any deer. I never put them back in the timber for that reason. Because the deer are coming out of the timber to eat in the food plots anyway, it makes sense to have one or more mineral stations set up on the edges of fields.

Building Ponds

"Most of the farms that Tiffany and I hunt in southeastern Iowa are fairly well watered. They contain numerous small streams and creeks, and in some cases large creeks, that carry quite a bit of water. However, even though you see deer crossing those creeks all the time, you very seldom see them drinking from the creeks. I think that's because they don't want to stop and expose themselves near those creeks where the woods are often fairly open.

"So I like to go into the timber near bedding areas on the farms we hunt with a Bobcat or dozer and push in small watering holes. I can't tell you how many times I've been out hunting and watched mature bucks get up from their beds and sneak over toward one of our small ponds during daylight to get a drink. They feel totally safe, and they do it with 100 percent confidence.

"I look for spots that already contain some sort of natural drainage where all of the water runs into a nearby creek. We have a lot of hilly country, and it's easy to find little crevices where the runoff goes down toward a creek. I'll pick my way through with my Bobcat and push out a small depression that will hold water. Some of these small watering holes that I've built are not more than 20 feet across. Most are very small, but the deer seem to love them.

In the early season when it's still warm out, bucks love a water source where they feel safe and secure, and they'll frequently come in for a drink during daylight.

"In recent years I've started putting in ponds right next to my small, isolated food plots back in the timber that we hunt over. The ponds and the food plots complement each other very well. These ponds don't have to be big. They can be anywhere from 20 to 30 feet across and not very deep. However, some are as deep as 15 feet because we have a good clay soil in Iowa that holds the water very well.

"I first learned about the importance of small ponds while hunting with a good friend, Ted Marum, in Buffalo County, Wis., in the early 2000s. Ted was an outfitter at the time, and it was the first year that Tiffany and I were trying to film some hunts for Realtree's *Monster Bucks* series. At the time, a lot of outfitters in Buffalo County built ponds in the timber to hunt over. And even though that was before I actually owned any land, that's where I realized how important ponds could be as a hunting tool.

"It's really hilly up in Buffalo County, and those guys would go in with a Bobcat and push up a little pothole in the timber. Those ponds were always so effective that we hunted them back then just like we hunt food plots today. They always produced more deer than the fields down in the bottoms did because hunting pressure was usually heavier on the field edges, and a lot of bigger bucks simply didn't come out during daylight.

Lee shot this great buck while hunting over a water hole in Buffalo County, Wis. Tiffany filmed the hunt.

"In the early season when it's still warm out, bucks love a water source like this where they feel safe and secure, and they'll frequently come in for a drink during daylight. And even during the rut, when you'd sometimes get those 70-degree days, a doe might come in to drink, and a big buck would be right behind her.

"I remember looking at one particular water hole several weeks before we actually hunted there, and I thought it was a great spot for a stand. So Tiffany and I went in and put up a stand setup (two stands so we could hunt and film together.) We returned to hunt there Halloween afternoon, and it was one of the first times that Tiffany had ever tried to film an actual hunt for Realtree. While hunting, we would always switch off — one day she would hunt, the next day I would hunt. It just happened to be one of the days I was hunting.

"Suddenly, we saw a big buck coming in to the water hole, and Tiffany nervously turned on the camera. I looked back at the screen on the camera, and everything was out of focus. I was really excited because I hadn't killed very many big deer at that time. She scrambled to adjust the lens, and everything came into focus just a few seconds before the buck put his head down to drink.

"Two little trees were blocking his shoulder, and I had one small window I could shoot through. I knew I would have to thread the needle, but I had been shooting a lot, and I felt confident I could make the shot. It was a 25- or 30-yard shot, and my arrow went right through the two little trees and hit him perfectly behind the shoulder. He ran through the middle of the pond and ran up the bank on the other side. Then he came running back toward us and piled up about 10 feet from our tree.

"I was ecstatic because that was the very first deer we ever killed on film specifically for a video. Tiffany and I ended up shooting a lot of great deer that year. As things turned out, it went on to be one of the best years ever for us. And that buck was a monster. He was basically a main-frame 10 with a triple brow tine on the right side, and he grossed just less than 170 inches. That hunt taught me a lot about the importance of small water holes in the timber.

Timber Management and Timber Stand Improvement

"Most of the farms we hunt contain heavy stands of hardwood timber. A few of those farms were originally used for grazing cattle, and the timber on those more open places is not as thick. Some of it is mature, and some of it is in various stages of growth. We have a lot of white oaks and other oak species that produce a good acorn crop most years. That can be good and bad. Any nutritious food is good for deer, but I really don't depend on those oaks as a primary food source.

"Instead, we use most of our timber stands on each farm as sanctuaries and bedding areas for our deer. But in years of too much rain where we can't get in the kind of crops necessary to carry the deer through to late winter, those acorns really help fill the void. And that's a good thing. On the downside, however, the deer stay pretty much in the timber feeding on acorns during those wet years, and that's not real good for our hunting — especially since we hunt mostly over food plots.

"Because the timber serves as a permanent sanctuary, we seldom hunt in the deep timber. One of the few times during the year that we ever go into the timber is in late winter — February or March — during shed season. Occasionally, we'll hunt the timber during the rut or in late season under special circumstances. I also hang most of my stands in late winter and try to do any improvement work that might be necessary, such as dozing out ponds sites or doing roadwork. Therefore, instead of depending on natural foods like browse and acorns, I depend on my food plots for hunting over and for giving our deer the extra year-round nutrition they need, although there is no question that natural foods are extremely important as well.

"I've never tried to sell any timber, and I would never sell any trees just for the money. The only time I would consider thinning any timber is if it made sense from a management standpoint. Or I might consider going in and thinning out some trees, like ironwoods, to open up certain areas and enhance the growth of young hardwoods. So far, we haven't seen a need to do that on any of our farms.

"In addition, we've never planted any trees like oaks, fruit trees or persimmons — mainly because I've been so busy doing other things — but that's something that we definitely might consider doing in the future. Right now, I'm putting most of my resources into food plots.

"Again, all of our standing timber on each farm is used primarily as a sanctuary for big bucks, and by keeping it strictly off limits to humans for most of the year, we feel like this is one of the most important things we do to hold bucks on our property and give them the sense of security they need to want to stay. It's all part of our low-impact hunting strategy.

Lee and Tiffany believe that a good entry and exit strategy is vitally important when hunting mature bucks.

What About Neighbors?

"When it comes to neighbors, I always assume the worst. I assume that there are going to be hunters on every one of my fence lines, and I plan my hunting strategies accordingly. I always ask myself, 'Can I tuck a food plot in the middle of the property somewhere to attract and hold deer, away from all roads and property lines?' If we have a lot of open land near any roads, we'll lease it out to farmers because we want our food plots socked in the middle. I definitely don't want any food plots near any boundaries or property lines.

"You'll often hear people say things like, 'Hey, it's right next to the Boy Scout camp where they don't do any hunting.' But what happens if the Boy Scout camp has all the good timber, and your land is mostly open? What if you've spent your life savings on the place, and the Boy Scout camp sells to an outfitter, and he pulls every deer that you could ever have off of your property onto his?

"Now you've got nothing. So you always have to assume the worst. You have to assume you're going to have terrible neighbors. If I go out to buy a piece, I want to buy the place that has it all or the place that has the potential to have it all, but never the place next to that place. And I always ask the question, 'How bad can the neighbors hurt me?'

"Even if the adjacent land is owned by a farmer who doesn't hunt, I've learned that all of that can change very quickly. What if that farmer sells to some hunters who shoot every buck they see, or what if he leases his land to an outfitter?

"After I figure out a good food plot strategy, the next question I ask myself is, 'Can I get in and out of the areas I plan to hunt in the mornings and afternoons without running off every deer in the neighborhood?' A good entry/exit strategy is so important, especially when you are hunting 5½-year-old bucks. A lot of hunters talk about it, but they don't practice it, and that's one of the biggest mistakes I see hunters making year in and year out. In truth, that might be the No. 1 mistake well-intentioned hunters make without even realizing it.

> After I figure out a good food plot strategy, the next question I ask myself is, "Can I get in and out of the areas I plan to hunt in the mornings and afternoons without running off every deer in the neighborhood?"

"You might get away with bumping a 3½-year-old buck and all of the other younger deer in the field several times, but never with a 5½-year-old. You bump him once, and you'll probably never see him again that season. Whenever I put in a small food plot where I plan to hunt, I always have multiple entry and exit trails leading in and out, and I usually have several tree stands or ground blinds set up in different locations so that I can hunt various winds.

"We go to extremes to set up our stand sites so that we can get in and out without bumping feeding deer. In certain cases, that might include setting up a ground blind on the edge of a food plot instead of using a tree stand. Or it might include building special roads or trails into an area that you can use for sneaking in and out without getting busted.

"Whenever I build one of these roads or trails, I always put an S-curve at the point where it enters the food plot. That way, feeding deer cannot look down the trail and see me coming 200 yards away. It also lets me sneak right up to the edge of the plot and see what's in it without getting busted. I keep the trails clear of leaves and other debris so that I can sneak in and out very quietly.

"I would much prefer to have a farmer next to me than a group of hunters practicing 'trophy management.' Even if that farmer and several of his family members hunt, they're only going to hunt a few days a year and shoot a few deer for the freezer. Probably more deer will get hit by cars out on the road in front of the property than that farmer or his family members

will shoot in a year's time. They simply don't care about shooting the big one.

"'Oh, it's deer hunting season,' he says, and he goes out and buys a license the day before, throws on his Carhart jacket and drives the timber with his friends and relatives on opening day. Chances are, he and his group will shoot whatever comes out — does, young bucks, occasionally a 2½-year-old 10-pointer — it doesn't matter. So the odds are good that a really big buck living on that farmer's property will make it through a three-day shotgun season.

"Occasionally, he will get a big one, but 90 percent of the time, the deer he shoots are going to be does, spikes and yearlings that have not gotten educated like the big boys. If a deer can make it on our property to 3½ and 4½ years of age, the chances are good that he'll be smart enough to make it to 5½ and 6½, even with some limited pressure by the farmer next door.

"I realize that my management philosophies are probably a lot different than those of most hunters around the country. In places like Pennsylvania, New Jersey or other Eastern states where every piece of timber had six guys sitting in it, it stands to reason that most of the deer they shoot are going to be 2½-year-olds. With some restraint and management, they might occasionally shoot a 3½- or 4½-year old. But when you take it to the next level and set your sights on hunting 5½- and 6½-year-old deer like we do in Iowa, you look at things from a different perspective. You don't want hunters sitting on every fence line.

"In most places, of course, it's a good idea to get together with your neighbors. Especially if there are a lot of hunters on relatively small tracts like 100 acres here and 50 acres over there. But in my case, I don't want any managers around me because I've found that most other 'trophy' hunters I talk to want to put in a food plot and shoot every 3½-year-old deer that comes into it. And even if they are like me, they really don't want be next to me. I do this for a living, and I spend every penny I make on my food plots. Likely, you're not going to outdo me.

"I probably have more food and better food, and I probably put more money into fertilizer than any neighbor will ever be willing to do. And it's likely that if there is a giant deer between our two farms, the odds are good that we're probably going to shoot it on our side because most people don't have 100 days to hunt during the season like Tiffany and I do, and most people aren't willing to put the resources into a piece of property that

> In most places, of course, it's a good idea to get together with your neighbors. Especially if there are a lot of hunters on relatively small tracts like 100 acres here and 50 acres over there.

we are. Let's face it: The odds of me shooting that buck over my neighbor are pretty good because I'm here all the time, I have cameras out everywhere, and I know what that buck is doing. I know where he's living, and I've probably figured out how to hunt him long before the season even opens.

"On the farm where we live, for instance, I think it's safe to say that there is a 200-inch buck on the place nearly every season. Everyone around us hunts, but there really aren't that many people, so the deer have a much better chance of growing older, especially superior bucks capable of growing 200-inch racks.

"In cases where you have someone 'managing,' however, how many people are going to pass up a 170-inch 4½-year-old and say, 'Oh, I'll let him go this year and see if I can get him to 190 next year?' Not very many. And a lot of those hunters who do make that claim can't pull the trigger fast enough when that 170 walks out for the first time.

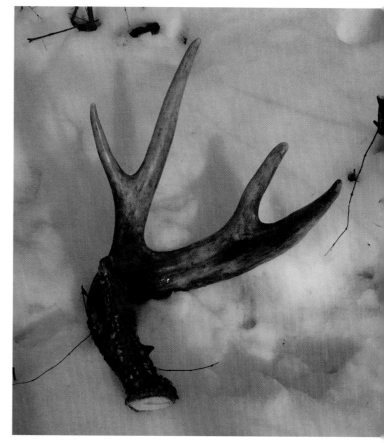

"For the most part, my neighbors on our home farm are meat hunters who slug-hunt. Each one of them is likely to shoot the first couple of deer he sees for the freezer. (Three is the legal limit in Iowa.) Chances are, those hunters are not going to target a genetically good deer with a giant rack. So a lot of our big deer with good genetics make it through the season. Now if those hunters were targeting our bigger bucks, they'd be a lot less likely to make it through the season. But those guys are just as likely to shoot a small 6- or 8-pointer as they are a really good deer.

"So my philosophy here in Iowa is different than with other people in most other places. I don't want other people around me managing. I don't care if my neighbors are average deer hunters. Now if that guy happens to be a serious hunter who says, 'I'm not going to be doing drives with my family like everyone else. I plan to go out in the woods and sit in the timber all day,' he'll have a much better chance of shooting one of the big deer in the area. Occasionally, a big one does get shot that way. But in most cases, if there really were a big deer around, we would have figured him out before bow season, hunted him hard on his normal pattern and probably killed him with an arrow long before shotgun season ever started.

"And like I said before, most hunters who say they are trying to manage for trophy bucks may get them to 4½ years of age, but they'll seldom get them to 5½ or older because they are not going to pass up those 4½-year-olds. And sometimes in the cases of the big 220- or 230-inch bucks that have been taken by hunters in Iowa and other places, it takes 7½, 8½ or even 9½ years to get that big. If a hunter has bought or leased property to manage, and if the guy is a good hunter and knows his property, that 4½-year-old buck is probably not going to get past him.

A Case in Point

"We own one very good farm where everyone around us manages for big bucks. A huge block of managed land surrounds that farm, and it's fun to hunt because you'll see a lot of really good deer and a lot of older deer because everyone who hunts around us is passing up younger bucks.

"In 2010, we had six bucks on that farm that we had targeted for our yearly hit list. They were all good genetic 5½-year-olds. By the end of the season, I had shot one of them, our good friend Brad Penny — a well-known major league pitcher currently playing with the Detroit Tigers — had shot one, and very predictably, our neighbors shot the other four.

"Every one of those bucks got shot because those hunters knew what they were doing. In reality, deer of that quality in a situation like that will seldom get beyond the age of 5½ because those guys are there all the time and they hunt hard.

"On our home farm, however, we also had several giant deer (5½ years old or older) that were on the hit list during the 2010 season. That season, I shot one good buck on the farm mentioned above and two management bucks on a different farm. Tiffany and I never even hunted on our home farm because we had already tagged out from hunting other deer. So those giant bucks on our home farm made it through the season by default because we never had time to target them specifically.

"On several of our other farms, all of the other bucks that we had on our hit list made it through the season as well for the same reason. And that was great for us, because we knew they would only be that much bigger the next season. But that kind of situation will never occur on our farm surrounded by trophy hunters because those guys won't allow it to happen.

"That farm has an unusually high number of bucks, including more mature bucks than you'll find in most other places. But the downside is that most of the bucks are 8-pointers with poor genetics because everyone is passing them up. There are also some good genetic 3½-year-olds in the 150-class range and they are being passed up as well. That's a good thing. It proves that the hunters who are managing the land are a step above most normal hunters who would be shooting every 3½-year-old they see.

"In most of the places where Tiffany and I hunt, some of the big deer that we target each year are going to make it through the season by default because we invariably end up tagging out somewhere else first as mentioned. We're fortunate to have a lot of big deer on all of our farms, but we can only hunt so many of them. Sure we'd love to shoot those 170-inch deer just like anyone else. And most of the time, we have them pretty well figured out before the season even starts, but they make it through the season nonetheless because we've already filled our Iowa tags somewhere else.

"So the difference in my management philosophy really is dramatic as compared with most people. Whenever someone comes up to me and says 'Hey, I want to manage my property next to you, so let's work together,' I don't say much, but in truth I'd much rather be next to Farmer Joe, who is only going to be out there hunting three or four days a year at most.

Dealing with Trespassers

"Wherever Tiffany and I go, people always ask us if we have any poaching problems. My answer is: 'If you have deer, you're going to have some trespassing and some poaching.' In recent years, shed poaching has become a real problem in Iowa and many other places. We've had some problems on some of our farms but not as many as you might think. All of our property has posted signs that say, 'This property is monitored 24 hours by surveillance cameras. If you need access, please call this number.' And people do call all the time.

"Quite often, we'll get calls from surveyors or the electric company asking us for permission to enter one of our farms. We want people to know that we have cameras out, and if somebody does get caught, word usually spreads like wildfire, and we've found that this is the best deterrent for keeping people out.

"That tells us that people are afraid to go in and trespass intentionally, although it does happen. I have a lot of my cameras well hidden up high and in places where you can't see them, and we have taken pictures of trespassers. Last year, we got some pictures of a trespasser stealing sheds. He was a local guy. When word gets around town that people have been caught, it really is a deterrent to future poaching. We also have several live 'smart' cameras set up where we can sit at home and watch what is going on in food plots and other places, and that helps as a way to monitor potential trespassers as well.

"Generally, the problems we've had with trespassers and poachers have been minimal, but we work very hard to protect our farms and the deer that live on them, and we have a lot of great people who help us out."

Lee and Tiffany monitor their properties 24 hours per day with trail and surveillance cameras.

2010-08-01 10:15:45 AM   M 2/3

LOW-IMPACT HUNTING: *A Must*

"**Y**ou can talk about strategies all you want, but it all boils down to keeping the pressure as low as possible on the land you hunt," Lee said. "That's the only way you'll ever be able to shoot a truly big buck (except possibly by blind luck). When I lived in Minneapolis, my friend Paul Landberg and I often went out to watch the deer that lived on the water-works property. They lived right in the middle of the city, and although we never got to hunt them, we watched them all the time. The property was fenced in to protect the water supply, and the deer population grew until the city finally had to do something about it — but we never got a chance to hunt there.

"People loved to watch the deer, and eventually they started throwing corn and other food over the fence. There were some good deer in there at that time. One was at least a 220-inch

7/26/2009   8:53 PM

The lack of pressure, combined with a good age structure and good food, ought to make it a lot easier to hunt big mature bucks anywhere in the wild.

buck. You could see those deer any time of the day, including a lot of big bucks. In the evening, they were always out walking along the fence line because they were totally unpressured. But they were not tame deer.

"They were as wild as any deer you might find in any wild setting, but they had never been hunted or pressured, so they were used to being around people. Watching those deer really left a lasting impression on me because they were on their feet all the time during daylight. Years later, when I had my own land to hunt on, I often thought about how those unpressured deer had acted and reacted to people. I thought, 'I want my hunting land to be just like that. It makes a lot of sense to try to manage my land like one big sanctuary. I want my deer to act like those deer at the water works. I don't want them to know they are being hunted. The lack of pressure, combined with a good age structure and good food, ought to make it a lot easier to hunt big mature bucks anywhere I hunt in the wild.'

"It seems like everywhere you go these days, you hear about special places where no hunting is allowed and where the deer are like those living in the water-works property — in other words, totally unpressured. Some guy will say, 'Oh, I've got a place next to the Boy Scout camp where no hunting is allowed.' Obviously, that's what you want to look for — a place next to a sanctuary where little or no hunting is allowed, and that's really the key.

"In reality, though, those places are few and far between — and hard to find. So why not make your place into one of those special sanctuaries. Your farm can be that piece of whitetail heaven if you want it to be, but your No. 1 strategy has to

be low-impact hunting. It's hard to achieve this when you don't control the land you hunt on. But even if you do control the land you hunt on, it's so easy to make the mistake of putting far too much pressure on that property.

"If you're hunting young bucks or does, you can get away with a lot of mistakes. But if you up the bar and set your sights on shooting a mature 5½-year-old buck, you might only get one chance to shoot that deer. If you blow that opportunity by spooking him even one time, you might never see him again, at least for the rest of that season.

"In truth, Tiffany and I talk to so many people who say they practice low-impact hunting, but they really don't. Putting too much pressure on the property they hunt might be the single biggest serious mistake that hunters make each year. We see this everywhere we go around the country. And in many cases, these hunters don't even realize they're doing it.

"I've read so many articles about the subject and heard so many people talk about it, yet people never seem to understand how serious this problem really is. Most people don't ever take the time to come up with a good plan for getting in and out of their stand locations. Whenever I go to places operated by outfitters or private landowners, they frequently show me their food plots and stand sites, and I always ask them how they get in and out without blowing the deer out. And they tell me, 'Well you really don't. You just have to kind of walk through them as carefully as possible.'

"If you blow a 3½-year-old out of a field once, he might come back in a day or two. He might come back the next day. You might even get away with spooking him two or three times during a period of several days. But with a mature 5½-year-old deer, you blow him out of there one time and the chances are good that you won't see him again that season during daylight.

"For example, say you've been getting lots of pictures of one or more 5½-year-olds at a certain secluded food plot that you know is going to be great. But the first morning out, say you walk into that field and bump those bucks in the dark without even realizing it. Chances are, you're going to spend the rest of that season wondering why you never saw them again and wondering what happened to them. This happens to hunters across North America so often that it's not even funny, and in most cases they don't even know it happened.

> In truth, Tiffany and I talk to so many people who say they practice low-impact hunting, but they really don't. Putting too much pressure on the property they hunt might be the single biggest serious mistake that hunters make each year.

"I'm not saying that if you do everything right it won't still happen to you once in a while. You can use scent control, hunt the wind, slip in undetected and do everything else right and still get busted by a doe that came up behind you or have something else happen that might spook that big buck you're after. But if you do everything within your power to hunt your farm with a low-impact frame of mind, the odds of seeing that big mature deer are going to be so much better.

Stay Out of the Timber

"Bumping a big buck one time might be all you get. There's nothing more important than keeping the pressure low on your farm. For you to see mature bucks during daylight and position yourself so that you might get a shot, those bucks have to feel safe and secure. If they don't, they simply won't come out during the daytime. That's why we seldom go into the timber.

"We do go into the timber on a very limited basis during shed season, and during certain circumstances, we might hunt the timber during the rut — when bucks typically throw all caution to the wind and cruise the hardwood ridges all day looking for does — or in the late season. But we keep it strictly off limits the rest of the time. We don't go into the timber during summer, and we seldom do it during the early part of fall.

"All of the timber on all of our farms is sacred ground. Every piece of timber is a sanctuary for our bucks. During hunting season, we have very specific ways to get in and out of our stands that are set up on the edges of our remote food plots, but that's it. No walking around. No looking for sign. No following trails to see if you can find any fresh scrapes. If you want to do that, do it during shed season in late February, but never do it during hunting season. Slip in, get in your stand, and slip out. That's it.

"Not that sometimes I won't be hunting a good stand and notice that all of the deer activity is over on the next ridge maybe 100 to 150 yards away. Yes, in that case I might get down and move my stand over 100 yards to adjust for those conditions. I'll slip over there as quietly as possible and pop up a new stand, but it's not like I'm out there the day before the season opens driving all over the property on my four-wheeler and putting up 10 stands. And even if I do move my stand, I'll still use the same way in and out. But that happens very rarely, and even then, there is always a chance of spooking that big buck I'm after without ever knowing it.

"When I do go into the timber during shed season, I ask myself, 'Has anything changed? Do I need to move any stands? Do I need to set up any new stands? I might be in those woods on a limited basis in March and April, but by the time the leaves are coming out in early May, I never hit those woods again until the next shed season. From May until January, there's seldom a person in any of our timber on any of our farms for any reason.

"I remember when I was younger, we would go places on public land, and I'd sit in a stand and get bored. By about 9 a.m., I'd decide to go walk around. That was probably a bad idea even back then, but today, based on the fact that we are

Lee and Tiffany consider the timber on their properties to be sacred ground, and they keep it off limits most of the year.

When you're hunting 5½- and 6½-year-old bucks, you can't risk spooking them out of an area.

hunting mature 5½-year-old bucks in the farm country of Iowa, it's something that you absolutely never do.

"Some people in certain parts of the country might be good at a spot-and-stalk style of hunting. And in places like Maryland or Pennsylvania, where you'll be lucky to see a 3½-year-old, it's possible to do with a rifle or shotgun. You might slip around and occasionally see a 2½- or 3½-year-old buck, but trying to shoot a mature buck with a bow in the kind of heavy timber we have is next to impossible. For every 10 times you try doing that, you're going to blow the deer out of there nine of those times.

"We even set up all our trail cameras on field edges and along roads and trails — where deer tend to congregate anyway — and never in the timber. That way, we can get to them very easily to check the cards without having to risk disturbing any deer in the woods.

Using S-Curves on Trails that Lead into Food Plots

"Obviously, you always have some kind of farm road or woods road leading into interior food plots large enough to get your equipment in and out. But to hunt certain stands in some of my more isolated fields back in the timber, I often build small roads or trails that lead to those fields so that I can get in and out without disturbing any deer.

"How many times have you been walking down a woods road that is as straight as an arrow toward a food plot and had one or more deer that were feeding in the field spot you and clear the field? It happens all the time. The deer might be 150 yards away, and they still see you.

"One trick I've learned to counteract that problem — and it has come in handy so many times through the years — is to make sure that all my trails leading into any food plots have one or more S-curves just before they empty into the field. By doing this, I can sneak along the trail and get right to the edge of the field — or over to a stand or ground blind a few yards to either side — without alarming any deer that might be feeding in the field.

"In fact, you might remember that this strategy worked perfectly for Tiffany and me on the afternoon of Oct. 3, 2009, as we were approaching the clover field that I had planted for Gnarles Barkley, the big buck profiled in Chapter 5. Because I had built an S-curve right where the trail enters the food plot, we were able to walk right up to the edge of the field late that afternoon to see if anything was out feeding. Sure enough, one buck was in that field — Gnarles. Three days later, I shot him with my bow from a ground blind I had set up a month earlier just a few yards from that S-curve in trail.

If big deer spend their days in relative isolation and safety, they're much more comfortable moving during daylight.

"If you've just bought or leased a new piece of property to hunt on, it's so tempting to want to get out there and walk the property, turkey hunt, look for mushrooms, put cameras out and drive around every free weekend you have. It's so tempting to want to check your food plots every weekend and drive around on your four-wheeler. Those things are a lot of fun to do, and they're all a part of the hunting experience. But if you do them on a regular basis, you're going to move all of your big deer right over to the next piece of property.

"It all goes back to low-impact hunting and what I was saying about those deer at the water works. They never had anyone in there driving around on four-wheelers or people walking around in there every weekend. They never had people going in there and setting up cameras. The water-works employees drove in, parked in the parking lot and never walked around in the woods where the deer lived. So the deer remained totally undisturbed. If you can get into your stand and get back out again without alarming the deer every time you hunt, it's a bonus. But that's the way it should be. That's the way it has to be if you want to shoot a 5½-year-old buck.

"Take opening day of shotgun season in my area, for example. In a lot of areas such as Iowa and Wisconsin, traditional deer drives are very popular among families and various groups of hunters. Although this style of hunting is a deeply seated tradition that thousands of hunters look forward to and enjoy every season, bow-hunting for mature bucks does not lend itself to putting that kind of pressure on deer.

"On opening day of gun season, these groups might do three or four drives on three or four pieces of property and see 100 deer. However, by the third day of shotgun season, you're lucky to see one deer in those same woods. And it doesn't really matter whether you're shooting at those deer or not. Just being in their woods is alarming to them. And after three days of being in those woods doing deer drives, it shouldn't be surprising to find that all of those deer will be gone. Doesn't that tell you something?

> No matter what I'm doing on the farm during any month of the year, I try to do it with as low an impact as possible. Everything really comes down to low pressure.

"Think about this: Doing deer drives on your property with a group of other hunters is really no different than several guys out driving around on four-wheelers, walking in the woods or hanging stands the day before the season opens. Suddenly, the deer start hearing all sorts of foreign noises like four-wheelers and trucks driving through the woods, doors slamming, loud voices and guns being sighted in, not to mention all of the strange scents that are filling the woods. They know something is up. They know hunting season has arrived.

"Sure, there are times that you have to get in the woods to check for sign and look for places to hang stands. But 99 percent of your scouting and stand hanging should be done in January and February, when the woods are wide open, and you can still see all the trails, rubs and old scrapes, which look just like they did back during hunting season in October and November. You should also be looking for sheds at this time of year, or maybe a month later in March.

"If you are discreet about the way you go about it, that doesn't bother the deer nearly as much at that time of year. It doesn't affect your property nearly as much as it does during hunting season because the land has roughly eight months to sit idle and recover, and those mature bucks that might have been

disturbed have all of that time to spend their days in relative isolation and safety, with no indication that they are being hunted.

"No matter what I'm doing on the farm during any month of the year, I try to do it with as low an impact as possible. Everything really comes down to low pressure. To us, that makes more of a difference than anything else we do. In Iowa, as well as many other parts of the Midwest, the deer are used to seeing farmers planting during planting season and harvesting their crops during harvest season. They're used to seeing tractors and trucks driving around in the fields.

"A lot of times, I'll check cameras that are set up on the edges of food plots from my tractor because the deer are so used to seeing farm equipment. I never put cameras back in the timber

because I don't want to disturb the bucks that might be bedded back there. Even during turkey season, we never go into the timber after turkeys. We always set up to hunt turkeys on the edges of food plots where we can get in and get out with minimal disturbance, just as if we were hunting deer.

"If a big gobbler is gobbling his head back in the woods somewhere, we don't go in there after him. The woods are off limits at that time of year. We might try to call him in from the edge of a food plot, but we leave the woods alone.

"And after about April 1, when shed-hunting season is over, we seldom go into the woods for any reason. During planting season, which lasts from spring until the end of August, we work in the fields and small food plots next to the timber, but we normally avoid going into the woods except on rare occasions.

"Last fall, I did break down and put up two stands on a farm that we've had for four years. That was the first time I had ever put stands in the timber on that particular tract. It took me that long — four years — to learn about where the deer were bedding on that property and how they were moving. It took me that long to feel confident about putting up two stands. I didn't want to go about it blindly, and after spending only a few days a year on that property looking for sheds, I finally figured out what I thought those deer were doing by the fourth year.

"As a result, I came up with a good place to put up two stands on a ridge. Both have a rock-solid place to get in and out without spooking any deer that might be in the field or in the timber. One of them is right on the edge of the timber only about 50 yards from a CRP field about 100 yards from the road. There is a well-used trail right in front of it, and with a west wind, I think I can sneak in and out without spooking any deer.

"We always try to have as low an impact as possible no matter what we are doing. If you dream about shooting a mature buck, you should too."

CHAPTER 9

TARGETING MATURE BUCKS

"I often think about my early days of bow-hunting," Lee said. "I wish I knew then what I know now. We had some fantastic spots to hunt in some of the metro areas of Minneapolis on golf courses and other places like that where the deer had never been hunted. And I'm sure there were some absolute giants on some of those places, although we never saw them.

"What would I do differently today? The thing that has really made a big difference to me when it comes to shooting bigger deer is paying a lot more attention to details — every little thing, including equipment, how we hunt certain areas and especially scent control. As far as scent goes, we do everything possible to eliminate our human odor. Today, we use all sorts of sprays and soaps, and we even use Ozonics, which uses ozone — charged particles of oxygen — to eliminate human odor from clothing. We have a scent closet that we run ozone in over our hunting clothes before each hunt.

It was a cold, snowy day just before Christmas 1994 when Lee shot this monster 11-pointer. He was hunting a 10-acre tract in Minnesota over a small clover patch, the only food in the area. With a gross score of 177 inches, the buck is still the biggest typical whitetail Lee has ever taken.

"Back when I first started hunting, we wore whatever and never worried about scent. We pumped gas at the gas station and went out into the woods with all sorts of odors on our clothing and bodies. And it showed, too, because it seemed that every little fawn we encountered would stand there and blow at us. I think that scent is probably the No. 1 thing that I didn't pay enough attention to in those days.

"Today, we go overboard to make sure that we are as scent-free as possible whenever we go out to hunt. In the old days, it seemed that every deer we encountered would blow at us, but now it very rarely happens. Now, when deer actually see us, they might blow at us, but we seldom get blown at when we are sitting in a stand.

"There are very few places you can go around the United States or Canada where the deer are not used to encountering some kind of human odor almost every day. And they can usually tell whether a human is 200 yards away or 20 yards away, or if someone was there yesterday or today. If you can at least eliminate enough of your scent to make the deer think you're 200 yards away instead of 20 yards — you're never going to get rid of it 100 percent — that's where the real difference comes in. So

Every time
you hunt a big
deer, you learn
something from
him.

at first light, and I really never got a good look at his rack. It was simply too early to see what size rack he had.

"A large sanctuary was located out in the middle of the swamp where no hunting was allowed, and lots of good deer were in there for that reason. The buck I had seen twice seemed to be headed for that sanctuary, so on the third morning, I got up at about 1 a.m. and headed out. By 2 a.m., I was headed into the swamp with a stand on my back. I got as close to the sanctuary area as I could, but I soon discovered that the only trees in there were short and scrubby. My stand wasn't five feet off the ground. The ground was covered with cattails, and even after daylight, visibility was limited.

"I sat there for three hours in the dark hoping to get ahead of that buck. Just like clockwork, he came in shortly before daylight, the same as he had done for the past two mornings in a row. But it was still too dark to shoot. He came right by me. Fortunately, he bedded down about 40 yards away. I could see him when he came by me, but I couldn't see my pins or my peep sight. Because he was bedded fairly close to me, though, I decided to just wait him out. I thought about grunting to try to get him to stand up, but I knew that he would eventually get up on his own if I just waited there patiently.

"I was fairly certain that he had bedded down, but I wasn't 100 percent positive because the cattails were so thick, and it had been so dark that he simply disappeared from my view. He finally stood up for a few minutes around 11 a.m. All I could see was his head, but I couldn't get a shot because the cattails were so high.

"He stood up again around noon. He walked around and stretched a little, ultimately offering me a shot at about 35 yards. I'll never forget the fact that when I released my arrow, my feet were about the height of his back when he was standing, because I was in such a small, scrubby oak. He turned out to be one of the biggest-bodied deer I had ever taken. By the time I found him and got him gutted, it was already getting dark that day. He was a huge-bodied 10-pointer that probably scored around 145 to 150 inches. I had walked back into that swamp nearly two miles, and now I was wondering, 'How in the world am I going to get this thing out of here?'

"I decided to go into town and buy a folding toboggan. Then I went back in there the next morning. It was a nightmare trying to get him out because I had been hunting by myself. I was constantly tripping over those large root heads that typically stick up in a swamp and twisting my ankles. I also bogged down numerous times in the mud and muck. I only got him about halfway out that day. I didn't have any money, so I spent the nights in my truck. I finally got him out of that swamp two days after I killed him. It had been an ordeal to get him out, but the sense of satisfaction I felt was huge.

"Sometimes you have to do things a little out of the box to shoot a big buck. In that particular case, I got up at 1 a.m. and sloshed into that swamp to hunt a spot where no one else would go. And it paid off. My friend Paul and I actually shot a lot of good deer back in those days because we were so passionate about hunting and so determined to be successful. He shot a giant back around that same time that scored about 180 inches.

"We worked hard at hunting big deer, and a lot of places we hunted were public hunting areas. We also spent a lot of time knocking on doors and looking for good places to hunt. So no matter where you live, you can always make things better if you're willing to work at it. It just takes hard work and dedication.

Taking it to Another Level: Targeting Mature, 5½-Year-Old Bucks

"Tiffany and I travel around a good bit, and we see a lot of hunting operations run by outfitters and private individuals. From what we've seen, I don't think a lot people put as much time and effort into planning their hunting strategies as they should. For us, though, since we're targeting 5½-year-old bucks — at least the ones that we know the ages of through previous sightings and trail-camera photos — I guess you could say that we're obsessed with doing everything we can to put the odds in our favor.

"Sometimes, a new buck will show up on a farm that we've never seen before, and it might be hard to tell exactly how old he is. If he's got that battleship body and big, bull-like head, it's sometimes hard to tell if he's 6½ or if he's 8½. Tiffany and I have even shot a few 4½-year-olds that we mistakenly thought were older, mature bucks.

"But you've got to be so careful in considering whether to shoot a deer like that. After all, if he's a 170-inch 4½-year-old, what's he going to be the next year when he's 5½? He might go more than 200 inches. For that reason, we've gotten very selective in shooting 4½-year-olds. We might shoot one of our 4½-year-olds if it happens to be a buck that needs to be removed from the herd for management purposes.

"For example, we've learned that on every piece of property we hunt, they'll be one — possibly more — very aggressive 4½-year-old that's so dominant he'll run off some of our more genetically promising bucks that we plan to put on the hit list in a year or two. It took us a while to get educated on what was happening. But when we figured it out, we knew that the only way we could keep the bucks with great potential on our property was to remove the more aggressive bucks that were causing the problem. A lot of those aggressive bucks were genetic 8-pointers. They get very gnarly when they get older, but they'll never grow a 190-inch rack.

"During the past few seasons, I've used one or two of my three Iowa tags to target and shoot some of these bucks to get them out of the herd. Each season, I always try to shoot one really good buck that is 5½ years old or older. After that, I'll consider shooting some of the other 5½-year-old bucks that we've identified as bucks that need to be removed from the herd. That's what I did in 2010 with two of my three tags, and I'm very glad I did it.

The Infamous Lakosky Hit List

"Our hit list is basically a list of bucks that we know and that we've watched for several years. We know that they're 5½ years old and that they're mature deer. We seldom put any bucks on the list that are younger than 5½ years old. It doesn't matter if the deer is a 130-inch 8-pointer, he'll be on the list when he hits 5½.

Of course, as mentioned, we sometimes encounter bucks that simply show up on certain farms each season. It's often hard to tell exactly how old some of these bucks are, and we sometimes have to make spur-of-the-moment decisions whether to shoot or not.

"We have a lot of big-bodied 8-pointers and even some 7-pointers that will never grow really big racks, even when they reach the age of 5½. And even though some of these deer are basically management bucks, they're all trophies to us because they're definitely mature bucks, and they're certainly not easy to kill. When you get one on the ground, with its huge head and neck, we know that they've reached their potential, so we're always happy to shoot a buck like that.

"For example, on the farm where I shot Gnarles in 2009, we had two really good 3½-year-olds; one we called Skyscraper and another we named Wally. They had great potential. In 2010, we had three 5½-year-olds on that farm that were very aggressive, including the big 9-pointer I shot. They were great deer. Two were in the 150s, and one was in the 160s. We put all three bucks on the hit list because we were afraid that if we didn't shoot them, they would run off Skyscraper and Wally. Fortunately, we shot all three bucks. Even though they were all great deer, as mentioned, they were still management deer. Going into

9/01/2009   6:43 PM   cuddeback.

The Lakoskys' annual hit list features bucks Lee and Tiffany have watched for several years and intend to target that fall.

the 2011 season, Skyscraper and Wally were 5½ years old and ready to be prime breeders.

"Because I have as many as 50 to 70 trail cameras out all summer, I get a lot of pictures of most of our older bucks. That gives me a chance to study them very carefully and try to determine how old they are. Some you know for sure, and some you just guess at, but you can usually tell which ones are mature. And those are the ones that go on the hit list. Sometimes, we'll add a buck to the hit list that shows up in December. And sometimes, we'll take a deer off the list if we study him and decide that he might need another year to turn into a really great buck.

"Whenever guests come in to hunt with us, I never tell them which bucks to shoot. They're always free to shoot any buck they like. But if they're hunting on a certain farm, I might show them a picture of a certain buck and say, 'This is a good deer that we're looking for. He's old and mature, and you're welcome to shoot him if you want to.' Of course, they might never see that deer.

"And that's the great thing about our hit list. We put the deer on it when they reach 5½ years of age, but so many of them slip through and get much older. If we have 20 deer on our hit list in any given year, we might only shoot six or seven of them.

"Occasionally, we'll also have one or more deer each season that are off limits to everyone. In Summer 2011, we had two 2½-year-olds that had already grown 170-inch racks. Those deer are one in a million, so we try to get them through to 5½. It's rare that you can do that, because if the neighbors see them, they're going to shoot them. And why wouldn't they? They're great deer, and I would have shot one like that myself a few years ago.

"In the case of a promising young buck that is off limits, I always tell my guests to be on the lookout for them. More often than not, they'll see one of them and even get good video footage of it. Three-and-a-half-year-olds are normally on their feet during daylight a lot more often than 4½- or 5½-year-olds, and that's why they're so much easier to kill. But if they make it to 4½, they tighten their core area, and you see them a lot less during the day. We normally have two or three very special deer that are off limits each season.

Reaching For the Stars

"It's not easy to shoot a 5½- or 6½-year-old deer. They're certainly not easy to kill, no matter what they've got on their heads. And whenever I tell people to, 'Shoot whatever you want,' I also tell them to think about the kind of deer they want before they

shoot. In other words, if someone decides to shoot a 3½-year-old, I don't want them to have any regrets after they see their deer on the ground.

"Two years ago, my cousin David Scovil came down from Minnesota to hunt with us. He had hunted with us in Iowa for several years in a row without shooting a deer, and each season I talked to him about what he should be looking for in the way of a mature buck. I told him he could shoot whatever he wanted to shoot, but I also talked to him about the pitfalls of shooting a 3½-year-old, because I didn't want him to be disappointed if he ended up shooting a smaller deer. Well, that's exactly what happened.

"On the farm where he was hunting, we had gotten several trail-camera pictures of a beautiful 3½-year-old buck. The pictures were head-on, and you couldn't see the rack all that well. We could tell that the rack was very palmated on one side, and it had a big drop tine. But we didn't really know that much about the deer because those two pictures were all we had.

"On the day of the hunt, Tiffany's brother Jason was filming with David. And wouldn't you know it, the palmated buck came out into the field in front of the stand they were in. David made a beautiful shot, and the deer ran a short distance and went down. The deer scored around 162 inches and had a very unusual rack. Who knows what it might have become if it had lived a few more years? But that was beside the point. We just wanted David to be happy with his deer.

"Jason told us that you could see the look on David's face right away when he walked up to his buck. It had looked so big on the hoof. Jason said you could tell what David was thinking by the look on his face: 'He's not as big as I thought.' For several years, David had seen pictures of some of the big bucks we'd been shooting, yet he never saw one himself while he was hunting. So that 3½-year-old understandably looked pretty big to him — until he got it on the ground.

"To add insult to injury, that same day Tiffany happened to shoot a big, mature 6½-year-old 9-pointer on a different farm. We had Tiffany's buck in the back of the truck when we pulled up beside David's deer. Next to Tiffany's deer, David's 3½-year-old looked much smaller, and he knew it. It had the very narrow neck of a 3½-year-old, and it just looked like a very young deer. Obviously a little embarrassed, David looked at me and said, 'Now I know exactly what you were talking about, Lee. I'll never doubt what you say again.'

"In fairness to David, he had never shot a deer like this before, and a 162-inch is a phenomenal deer just about anywhere in North America. 'You should be super-proud of that deer,' I told him. 'Just because we hunt older deer doesn't take away from your buck in any way. It's an awesome buck. And hey, we might never have seen your deer again. We only had two pictures of him, so we didn't know a lot about him.'

> It's not easy to shoot a 5½- or 6½-year-old deer ... no matter what they've got on their heads. And whenever I tell people, "Shoot what you want," I also tell them to think about the kind of deer they want before they shoot.

"David learned a big lesson that day. It's something we all have to go through as hunters. It's part of the learning process. I had to learn the same lesson myself. It's hard to tell people in so many words, and it's something that you almost have to experience firsthand before you understand it.

"I told David, 'I've got a wall full of deer like that, and I'm proud of every one of them. But now, Tiffany and I have simply raised the bar in our own personal hunting, and now you understand what I was trying to tell you.'

"Most 3½-year-old bucks are simply not as big as hunters think they are. Unless a deer looks like he's going to tip over because his rack is so huge, he's probably not the buck you want to shoot — that is, if your goal is to shoot a truly mature buck. And when you do actually see a 170-inch deer, he'll look so big that there's no question. He'll take your breath away. He'll actually looks like he's going to tip over because his rack is so enormous.

"Not that they aren't great deer, but when you see a 150- or a 160-inch deer, you'll often think it's a giant, especially if it has the typically smaller body of a 3½-year-old. But when you see a 170-inch deer that has a body to go with his rack, your heart will skip a beat. You'll know without question that he's the buck you want to shoot.

"When people come here to hunt with us, they often ask, 'What deer should I shoot?'

"As mentioned, I always tell them the same thing I told David. 'You shoot any deer you want to shoot. But just be careful, because I don't want you to have any regrets if you shoot one that turns out to be smaller than you think it is. You came here to hunt, and I don't want you to have to worry about every deer you see. So you shoot whatever size buck you'll be happy with. Mainly, just try to have a good time and enjoy your hunt.'

> You need a variety of good food sources on your land to hold deer, and I've learned through the years that big bucks remember where the good food sources are located, even if they've been away from that property for three or four years.

"If I see a promising young deer that I think is going to grow a 200-inch rack in a year or two, I probably won't put an inexperienced hunter on the farm where that deer lives. I'll probably put him somewhere else, where there are other bucks that don't have that kind of potential. Three-and-a-half-year-olds are so easy to shoot compared to older bucks because you see them much more often. In fact, probably 90 percent of the deer taken by hunters who book hunts through outfitters are 3½-year-olds because they're so much easier to shoot than older bucks.

"That's why I don't trust neighbors who come to me and tell me they want to manage for so-called 'big' bucks. To most people, 'trophy management' means putting in a food plot and shooting every 3½-year-old that comes out in the field. But for Tiffany and me here in Iowa, and in other places we hunt, such as Kansas, we deliberately target mature bucks that are 5½ and older.

Best Time of Year to Hunt?

"You need a variety of good food sources on your land to hold the deer, and I've learned through the years that big bucks remember where the good food sources are located, even if they've been away from that property for three or four years. If a young buck fawn is raised in an area with good food, even if he leaves that area or gets run out as he gets older, he's always going to remember where that good food source was located. And he's very likely to come back to check things out during the rut when he's 4½ or 5½ years old, especially when food gets scarce in other areas.

"Or, he might visit your farm during early season or late season, when your food plots are the only good food source available. And when you get him around all that good food, there's a good chance that with all of the deer in your fields in the early and late season that he might decide to stay there or at least come check things out during the rut. It pays to provide good food for so many reasons, and we go to great lengths to make it happen on every one of the farms we hunt.

"Even though you've got a lot of food on your property, you might hunt that food early and late in the season, but it's a different story during the rut. Your bigger bucks are going to be in the timber, where all the does are bedding. They might come by and check a field early in the morning or late in the day, but most of the does are going to be in the woods during the middle of the day during the rut.

"You might get some action in the fields, but in most cases, the does avoid the fields because they know if they step out into the open during the rut, a lovesick 2½- or 3½-year-old buck is going to be waiting close by, and he's going to run her right back into the timber. So even the does often go into hiding during the rut.

"I've had far better luck during the rut getting on the hardwood ridges just inside the timber close to where the does are bedding. You should know where all the beds are from shed hunting in March. If there's a little snow on the ground in March, you can see the beds very distinctly, as well as the trails leading to them.

> Instead of weights and body sizes, I like to concentrate more on that giant cinder-block face and big neck on the deer I hunt. To me, that's a sign of maturity.

"Generally, though, if we're going to shoot a big one on one of our farms, it's not going to be during the rut. That's not our best time to hunt big mature bucks. It might be the time when you have the most fun, because there's so much grunting, snorting and chasing of does going on, especially on the farms we hunt because we hold so many deer.

"If we're going to shoot a real big one, it's almost always going to be during the first 10 days of October, or it's going to be late in the season, when it's really cold and nasty. Not that we don't occasionally shoot a big buck during the rut, but not nearly as many as we do during other times of the season.

"On a national average, I'd say most people love to hunt the rut, but most of the deer they end up shooting are 2½- or 3½-year-olds that are out chasing does. In our area, the kind of big old deer we want to shoot are usually not out in the fields chasing does. Instead, they wait back in the timber and take the does when they are ready.

"An old, mature buck will often take a doe out into the middle of a large field and hide in a clump of brush. Or he might take her out in an overgrown CRP field. When the buck and the doe are in a place where the old buck won't be bothered by younger, more aggressive bucks trying to take his doe away from him, he might stay in that spot for three or four days with very little moving around.

"Then, when that buck is finished with one doe, it usually doesn't take him very long to find another doe. In places such as our Kansas farm, where the deer numbers are not as high, the bigger bucks might have to do a lot more moving around during the rut to find a doe. But in Iowa, where we have high deer numbers and hundreds of does, it's like a deer factory, and it only takes the big boys 15 minutes to find another receptive one. We've found that on most of the farms we hunt in Iowa, the big

nity to shoot one of them. In my opinion, you've got to get them on food — either early in the season or possibly late in the season. During the rut, your chances are going to be a lot slimmer because so many other younger bucks are getting so aggressive, and a buck like Gnarles or the big 240 are not going to be around where those younger, more aggressive bucks are constantly fighting for dominance. During the hunt for Gnarles Barkley, I figured I had to make a plan and try to kill him early, and the only way I could do that was over food. And in that case, the plan worked."

Tiffany's View

"During the past few seasons, I've gotten to the point where I've started looking for specific deer to shoot," Tiffany said. "I never used to do that in the past, but the idea of hunting one certain buck has become very appealing to me. Several seasons ago, I more or less targeted a buck that we called Turkey Foot. No other buck would do. I wanted to shoot Turkey Foot in the worst way. I hunted him for nearly a month and saw him numerous times, but I never could get a shot at him. That season, I ended up shooting a big 8-pointer.

"We have so many great deer to hunt in southeastern Iowa, and I also tend to key in on certain farms that I like to hunt more than others. Certain stands in certain spots have more appeal to me because of the beauty of the area or simply because I might like a certain stand. I passed up several really good bucks in 2010, and I'm really hoping to see several of them during the upcoming 2011 season.

"One buck in particular that I hope to see is a deer I missed in 2009 from a stand that we call the Candlestick Stand. Lee was filming me, and I was back at full draw ready to shoot, and he said, 'No don't shoot. Yeah, maybe you should. No he's not quite big enough. What do you think? Yes go ahead.' I released my arrow and shot right under him.

"We call these deer 'betweeners' because they are probably 4½ years old, and they have great racks, but they're not quite big enough to shoot. They really need another year, but they are very tempting nonetheless. At any rate, it was probably a good thing that I missed him. We never saw him during the 2010 season, but we found his shed in early 2011, and we know he's a real stud now. He's living right in the same area where I missed him in 2009, and I'd really love to get another chance at him one of these days.

> During the past few seasons, I've gotten to the point where I've started looking for specific deer to shoot. I never used to do that in the past, but the idea of hunting one certain buck has become very appealing to me.

"Like Lee says, I've learned that it's a lot harder to shoot a 5½-year-old buck than it is to shoot a 3½-year-old. You have to be smarter and take all the important steps in making sure that everything is right. The wind has to be right, your clothes have to be right, and you really have to take the time to get to and from your stand without disturbing the woods around you. In Iowa, we're able to hunt older bucks successfully because we're in the woods so many days during the season.

"As a whole, though, I'm a lot like Lee in that we both get so much enjoyment in growing these big bucks. It's not just about killing them when they get old enough. It's about watching them for several years as they grow up. It's about getting trail-camera photos, finding their sheds, naming them and wondering if they've survived the season. That's the real magic in managing for big deer.

"It's about wondering how big they're going to be the next year, wondering where they go at certain times of the year and if your hunting strategy is going to work. That's the real challenge for us in hunting older deer. And if you do get lucky and shoot one in the end, that's what makes it so exciting and satisfying.

"Sometimes when you do shoot one, you say 'Oh,' and you almost feel a sense of sadness, because you know you're not going to see him again the next time you're out in the woods. At the same time, there's nothing like the feeling you get when you do everything right and you end up with a nice trophy buck.

"During the first two years that we hunted on our home farm after we moved to Iowa, we shot some high-scoring young deer that were mostly 3½-year-olds. Then during our third year, we set our sights a little higher and decided to go for some older deer. That was when we discovered that just about every ridge on the property was controlled by a highly aggressive younger buck. Most of them had gnarly 8-point racks.

"These deer were what we would later call management bucks. That is, they never grow great sets of antlers, and they need to be removed from the herd. But these gnarly management bucks were definitely dominant deer, and we soon realized they were running off some of our older bucks that had the best potential. So we learned that we had to start shooting some of these deer if we wanted to keep some of our better bucks on the property.

"One buck in particular, a buck that we named Old Crappy because of his gnarly and unattractive 8-point rack, came running in just about every time I rattled. Lee said, 'You've got to shoot him' and I said, 'I don't want to shoot that deer.' He was a little beast that probably didn't score 120 inches tops. When I finally did shoot him, one eye was all puffed out from fighting, and his other eye was swollen almost shut, but he was still looking for a fight. You have to shoot bucks like that if you want to keep some of your older, less aggressive bucks with bigger racks on your property.

"During the 2010 season, I was filming with Nate DeLong of Scent-Lok on our home farm when we had a gnarly 8-pointer come in that probably scored 100 inches at the most. He was a huge-bodied brute of a deer with a very small rack, and we both went to turn around, and he saw us and spooked. Nate said, 'That was the ugliest deer I've ever seen,' and we agreed. But I said, 'It doesn't matter what kind of rack he has. You have to shoot him if you see him again because he's a mature buck, and he's one of those deer that we have to get out of the herd.'"

> It's about watching them for several years as they grow up. It's about getting trail-camera photos, finding their sheds, naming them and wondering if they've survived the season. That's the real magic in managing for big deer.

CHAPTER 10

SEASONAL STRATEGY

"I think it's so easy for a lot of hunters to get complacent," Lee said. "They say, 'Oh, I've got plenty of beans out there, or at least the farmer does. If I can keep hunting over those beans, the big buck I'm after is bound to come back sooner or later, even though I haven't seen him in five or six days.' But those hunters are only fooling themselves. It's not the same when those beans start going away or when the farmer takes them off, because you've got nothing unless you have another good food source that the deer can move to.

"If you've got good food in early season and good food later on, your chances of keeping those deer on your farm are so much better. In late season, it's not uncommon for us to see 200 deer in one field. Of course, those deer are not all living there. They're coming in from miles around, but a lot of times you can relocate some of those deer — especially some

of the older bucks you might want to shoot next season. And if a big one comes in, you might be able to keep him on your property, because he's got everything he needs to get through the coldest part of winter.

"Quite often, we'll see a lot of these unfamiliar 5½- and 6½-year-old bucks in late season, and a month later we find their sheds. Then, a month or two after that, there they are in velvet, still on the property. They came to our property following a food source, and they liked what they saw. So they decided to stay because they felt safe and secure.

Early Season the Lakosky Way

"Without question, early season is definitely my favorite time of year to be in the woods hunting. It's also the time when we shoot most of our big bucks. If we're going to shoot a big deer, it's probably going to be early in the season or late. More often than not, it's going to be early, especially since we hunt exclusively with archery gear at that time of year. We'll normally shoot our best deer within the first 10 days of the season in early October.

"And that makes sense, because they're still on their late-summer feeding patterns, and they're still pretty much following their summer routines. The rut hasn't started kicking in yet, and they haven't been bothered by a lot of hunting pressure, so they're still fairly visible. In Iowa, archery season opens Oct. 1. If you have the right setup, I'd even go so far as to say our early-season hunting is good right up until the end of the month. But to keep it that good, and to hunt the older age-class deer that we hunt, you have to be able to get in and out of your stand without spooking the deer."

Tiffany agreed.

"Not only has early season always proven to be our best chance for shooting a big buck, but I love hunting early in fall when it's so pretty outside and the temperatures are still fairly mild," she said. "It's not cold yet, and it's such a beautiful time of year to be in the woods.

"We have a few morning stands that we hunt during the early season, but we generally see a lot more activity in the afternoons. When we're at home, I usually get to my stand in midafternoon and sit for three or four hours. But we're always trying to do a million other things at home during the middle of the day, too.

"Taking care of business, answering phone calls, doing numerous chores on the farm and taking care of guests who are hunting with us are all very time consuming, so sometimes it's a little harder to get out and hunt when we want to. That's why it's nice to be away from home from time to time

> Not only has the early season always proven to be our best chance for shooting a big buck, but I love hunting early in fall when it's so pretty outside and the temperatures are still fairly mild.

Lee and Tiffany use rubbing posts in many of their food plots. That tree usually becomes an immediate signpost — that is, a scent-marking tree.

during th_____ trying to do all of those
_____ more hours in a stand actually

_____ovember arrives, that's when the older deer
usually disappear," Lee said. "You'll see bucks chasing does, running after them and grunting at them, but those deer are likely to be 2½- or 3½-year-olds. The older deer in our area don't

typically chase does like the younger bucks do. They simply find them and take them when they are ready. But they don't chase them all over the woods like the younger bucks do.

"Not that we don't ever see any big ones during the rut. Sometimes, you'll see them out cruising around when they've just finished with one doe and are out looking for another, so we do occasionally shoot a big deer during the rut. But not very often. Ninety percent of the deer we shoot are taken early or late in the season, and 70 percent of those are taken in early season.

"So early season really is my favorite time to be out bow-hunting. By the time our season starts on Oct. 1, I've been watching the deer all summer, and I know where they're feeding and bedding. I've been studying trail-camera photos, and I know which deer are on our hit list. I know our best chance is going to be during those first few days right after the season opens.

"I hear stories all the time from hunters who tell me, 'I was watching a certain buck all summer long feeding in my bean field, and I had a good stand setup, but as soon as October rolled around, he disappeared.' That deer didn't disappear. He just changed his feeding habits because the beans that hunter was watching turned yellow and dried up.

"When that happens, if you don't have a good food source for your buck to shift over to, you won't see him again, because he's going to be on that next good food source on the farm across the road. That's why our smaller, more remote food plots are so important, and that's why we've had such good luck hunting them. As soon as the beans start going away, we have clover, winter wheat, Buck Forage Oats and other greens in our smaller food plots that the deer will automatically shift over to.

"When you have your own place to hunt on and you can design your own food plots, you more or less control your own destiny. You can say, 'OK, I have a big bean field that the deer will be moving off of around the Oct. 1. So if I plant some lush clover or oats in a couple of small, remote food plots back in the woods, those deer will naturally switch over to that new food source.

Ninety percent of the deer we shoot are taken early or late in the season, and 70 percent of those are taken in the early season.

"Then all you have to do is make sure you can get in and out of your stand without spooking any deer. That is so important. You can't afford to let those big deer know you are there. If you can do that, you're chances of seeing the buck you've been after are excellent. That's exactly how we've been able to shoot a lot of our big deer, including one of my biggest and best bucks ever, Gnarles Barkley (See Chapter 5).

"I had watched Gnarles all summer feeding in a large bean field with several other bucks, and I specifically went and dozed in a small clover field just for him. I knew those beans would no longer be a prime food source in October, so I purposely planted that clover field 300 yards from the bean field right in the middle of the timber where I knew he had to be bedding during the day. Whenever he came out of the timber into the bean field, he always used the same trail, so I had a good idea of where he was bedding. I put the clover field on the other side of that timber because I figured it had to be close to where he was bedding during the day, and I knew he couldn't help but find it.

"I dozed that field during summer, and limed it and fertilized it with great care. I nurtured it and pampered it like was the most important food plot I had ever planted. By Oct. 1, that clover was lush and thick — 12-inches tall, with no weeds in it. And sure enough, by late September, we never saw Gnarles on the bean field again. Then, the first day in early October that Tiffany and I went to check that field, he was there feeding in the clover. I didn't kill him that day, but I did kill him in the clover a few days later when the wind was right.

A Winning Early-Season Scenario

"We know that our deer like to feed and congregate in the larger fields at night. This is pretty typical of deer everywhere. Even if they're not feeding all that much around daylight, they're socializing or just hanging out around the edges of our larger food plots containing corn and beans in the mornings. Within an hour of daybreak, however, almost all the deer in the field are going to start working their way back into the timber, where they routinely bed down for the day.

"Because our smaller food plots containing clover, wheat, oats and other desirable greens are tucked into remote spots back in the woods, deer will often hit those middle fields in the timber as they are coming off the larger fields and moving toward their daytime bedding areas. Because we strive so hard to keep the pressure off our deer, they feel safe and secure in those secluded food plots.

"If you can sneak into one of those smaller food plots in the timber and get set up in your stand an hour before daylight without alarming any deer, there's an excellent chance that you might intercept one of those big bucks as he is coming off the larger field and moving toward his bedding area. The key is for that buck to feel so confident in his surroundings that he'll still be out 30 minutes to an hour after first light. If he's experienced the least bit of pressure, he certainly won't expose himself in the open.

"As far as early-season tactics go, this strategy has worked extremely well for us the past few years. As a result, we've taken some of our best mature bucks during the first 10 days or two weeks of archery season. This might sound a little boastful, but killing a 3½-year-old buck is relatively easy compared to killing

> Because we strive so hard to keep the pressure off our deer, they feel safe and secure in those secluded food plots.

a 5½-year old. In Chapter 8, I mentioned that if you're going to kill a mature 5½-year-old buck or older, like Gnarles Barkley, you're going to have to do it over food early in the season or late.

"Your chances of getting him during the rut are going to be very low because he's not going to be around. He's going to be lying low, avoiding those other bucks, or he'll be with a doe in some remote spot. Many of the older bucks we hunt are very non-aggressive, and they won't come to rattling horns, grunting or any kind of calling. I've learned that the hard way. If you try to grunt one in, they'll often go the other way. They're smart. They're survivors. They don't want anything to do with younger, more aggressive bucks that are itching for a fight.

"Food is the only real sensible option in being able to get close to older bucks during daylight. Find out what they're eating, and hunt them close to the source. Better yet, plant your own food plots on your own land, and you'll have a lot more control of the situation. When you have the food source, a low-impact hunting strategy will be vital if you plan to target an older buck.

Using Rubbing Posts

"We use rubbing posts in most of our larger food plots and also in some of our smaller plots in the woods. Often, I'll leave a single small tree out in a new food plot that I'm just putting in. That tree usually becomes an immediate signpost rub; that is, a scent-marking tree. Because many of my larger food plots were originally old fields with no trees in them, in those situations, I'll place a rubbing post in the ground near my critical stand locations.

"Basically, my rubbing posts are roughly 8-foot-long cedar or hardwood posts 5 or 6 inches in diameter placed 2 feet in the ground within 30 yards or so of a tree stand that will be just inside the tree line on the edge of the food plot. I always attach two or three freshly cut branches to the posts with fresh leaves on them just before the season or a few days before a hunt. I drill large holes into the posts, place the branches in the holes and then put screws through them so they can't be dislodged. I might freshen up the rubbing posts with new branches as the season progresses. They'll stay green for several weeks, and I like to use cedar or other preferred branches from trees that the deer like.

> Having a rubbing post close to your stand is a great way to entice the deer to get within bow range, especially if they are across the field or just entering the field from the woods.

"Because these rubbing posts serve as a community signpost, every buck coming through the area will come by and check them out. If there are a bunch of deer out in the field, the bucks love to come over, posture up and rub the post, or use one of the branches as a licking branch and leave his scent. They often make scrapes under each branch, and every buck approaching will come in and work that scrape. Or they might walk over and hit another scrape along the tree line. Having a rubbing post close to your stand is a great way to entice the deer to get within bow range, especially if they are across the field or just entering the field from the woods.

"Another advantage of having a rubbing post out in front of your stand is that it can be a distraction, just like a decoy. If one or more bucks come out, or if a giant happens to come out, those bucks will definitely be preoccupied with the post long enough to give you time to evaluate that big buck's antlers and set up for a shot. Rubbing posts are great hunting tools, and they've worked well for us through the years.

What About the So-Called "October Lull?"

"In a lot of ways, that can almost be clichéd. People often think that the deer simply stop moving for a period of time in late October just before the rut kicks in. But in truth, the deer

185

again, and going to the same spot to hunt every time you go in, it's likely that you're bumping the same deer again and again. In that case, those big bucks get educated in a hurry.

"Although I'll often go to one spot and sit all day during the rut, it's nice to be able to see some different scenery once in a while. This is especially true if things are slow in the spot you're hunting and you know the action is happening somewhere else. Obviously, you're not going to see as many deer in the timber during the rut as you would if you were hunting over a food plot in the early or late seasons, so I'll sometimes go to a good morning spot and hunt until noon on one farm, and then slip out and go to another farm and hunt there in the afternoon.

"Any stand I hunt in the morning should always serve as a good all-day stand, and during the rut, I might want to sit there all day, especially if I'm seeing some good action. I usually hunt long hours — often all day. But there are some stands that are simply better afternoon stands, and that's the reason why Tiffany and I sometimes change locations after the morning hunt if we're not seeing much action.

> Any stand I hunt in the morning should always serve as a good all-day stand, and during the rut, I might want to sit there all day, especially if I'm seeing some good action.

"Occasionally, I'll set up on a field edge or along a pipeline easement in spots where I can see a long way where I might spot a big buck cruising for does. He might be cutting across the field or the pipeline, and in that situation, I might try rattling or grunting to try to get him in close enough for a shot. But normally at that time of year, I'll spend a lot more time in the timber. Again, it's one of the few times of the year that I would ever think about going into the timber.

"The rut is the one time of year where it really pays to have numerous farms to hunt on and numerous stands set up for just about any condition. We have more than 200 stand setups on the various farms we hunt — double stands; one for the hunter and one for the cameraman — so we have a lot of options. Our main goal is to try to keep things as fresh as possible at all times. Whenever you do go into the timber, even with the right wind, you never know how many deer you might be bumping.

"So even when we do hunt the timber, we rarely go back to the same stand or even the same farm more than twice a week. Unless I happen to be on a specific deer that I'm actively looking for, I might not get back to a farm that I hunted on any given morning for quite a while. Rotating around the way we do on different farms really keeps the pressure to a minimum on any one place.

"Scrapes and rubs are important, but you don't necessarily always know which bucks made them. However, it really doesn't matter. If you did your homework during shed season, you should know where all the big scrapes are located in the timber, and usually you'll find that they're often in the same spot from year to year. The same is true with big rubs. If a big rub is made one year, it'll often get hit again the next year, sometimes by the same buck. If I see an area with a lot of sign during shed season that looks super good, I'll check it out and get a stand up in that location right away.

There's nothing like being in your stand before daylight when everything is still dark and quiet, and you hear that "eenh, eenh, eenh," of a grunting buck running by you.

"I won't go back in there until the rut. That's when I find out if those scrapes are still being used or if that big rub is still being hit by a large buck. Usually they are. But I don't ever walk around to find what the deer are doing while I'm hunting. I should already know that based on what I learned during shed season."

Tiffany agreed that the rut is one of the most exciting times to be in the woods.

"There's nothing like being in your stand before daylight when everything is still dark and quiet, and you hear that 'eenh, eenh, eenh,' of a grunting buck running by you," she said. "I do some rattling and some calling under certain circumstances during the rut, but not a whole lot. I've had a lot more luck just sitting quietly during the rut and letting the deer come by me naturally. If a buck is already with a doe, chances are you're not going to call him away from her. You have to try at least some rattling and grunting during the rut, and I've had very good luck with snort-wheezes, but it's amazing what you see when you're sitting quietly.

"During the rut, we have our morning spots and our evening spots, and we very rarely hunt all day. Generally, we hunt just inside the timber in the mornings and the field edges in the afternoons."

Attracting Other Mature Bucks During the Rut

"During the rut, if a big deer knows where all the does are bedding on your farm, he might go check them out from time to time even if he doesn't live on your property," Lee said. "We have that happen every year. And every year in the late season, we see bucks that we've never seen before. That's even more reason to keep the pressure on your farm as low as humanly possible.

"In Chapter 9, I mentioned the fact that young bucks often leave the home property where they were born. Sometimes they are run off by their mothers or by other bucks, and sometimes they naturally move to a new home range. But if they were raised on a farm that offered good food and goods protection, they don't forget, even after several years. So they might return to their old stomping grounds during the rut to look for does, or they might return in late season when food is scarce in other places.

"Obviously a 5½- or 6½-year old buck will probably not return to his old range if the farm where he was raised experiences heavy hunting pressure. He'll avoid that farm at all costs, no matter how many does are there or no matter how good the food is. Or if he does happen to return for those reasons, he'll only do it under the cover of darkness, and seldom come out during daylight hours.

"On the other hand, if he feels safe and secure on your farm because of good food, low hunting pressure and because he has so many undisturbed places in the timber to spend the day in, the chances of seeing him during daylight increase dramatically.

Late Season

"In Iowa as well as much of the Midwest, late-season hunting is no big secret. If you have the food, you're going to have the deer. I can remember how tough it was to hunt late season in Minnesota when I was growing up. If you were lucky enough to shoot a doe back then, you were really doing something. After gun season opened, the deer in northern Minnesota simply did not move. So late season was an impossible time for me back in those early days. But now it's easy to see just how critical food is at that time of year. Wherever the food is, that's where the deer are going to be.

"And I think this rule could apply to most places around the country, although it's a lot more critical in the colder climates where the deer have to withstand days and even weeks of sub-zero temperatures and deep snow. In the South, they might go hungry for a while, but they'll probably survive the winter months. Here in the Midwest, and in many of the northern states and Canada, if they don't have a good late-season food source, they can easily die.

"So often, your late-season success is going to depend on how much pressure you put on your farm or hunting land during the regular season. Say you've already been through nearly three months of hunting — the bow season, the gun season, everything. Say you applied no more pressure than just normal farming activity, and you were super careful about your entries and exits while actually hunting. If the deer you were after didn't realize they were being hunted, it's very likely that they'll come out during daylight on those late-season food sources.

"However, if you and your friends conducted deer drives in your timber every day during shotgun season, don't plan to see the bucks you were hunting in your late-season food plots during daylight. You'll see the younger bucks and maybe the 3½-year olds, but when you've educated those older bucks and put even a small amount of pressure on them, they're not going to come out during the day.

"If you haven't been overly aggressive during the previous 90 days, and if you've hunted your property with extreme care and caution, it's really pretty simple. If you hunt over a good food source in late season, you're going to see some big bucks, especially if it's cold and snowy. The worse the weather, the more likely you are to see a big buck.

So often, your late-season success is going to depend on how much pressure you put on your farm or hunting land during the regular season.

"By now, deer are in their worst shape of the year because they're still worn down after the rut. They were with does during the peak of the rut, and they haven't eaten much. Now, if they're going to survive the next couple of months, they're going to have to find a good food source. All they really want to do at this time of year is eat and rest.

"So the smartest thing you can do from opening day forward is to make it a priority to keep the pressure on the farm you are hunting as low as possible. Of course, whenever we target a specific buck, we sometimes hunt the same farm and even the same stand a lot more than normal. We might hunt the same area every day for several days in a row. But if we do, we always make sure the wind is right, we always use maximum scent control, and we always go to extremes to make sure our entries and exits do not spook any deer.

"If you just have one farm to hunt, keeping the pressure as low as possible can be a hard thing to do, because your natural inclination is to want to get out there and hunt as much as possible. You'll probably want to hunt during early bow season. If you don't fill your tag early, you'll definitely want to hunt the rut, and you might even want to hunt during shotgun season and beyond that.

"So it stands to reason that by the time late season arrives in late December, the deer on your place probably know they are being hunted. Any big bucks on your place that have not been bumped and run off will probably be almost 100 percent nocturnal. Even though they'll be looking for food in late December or early January, you're probably not going to see them during the day, unless you have gone to extremes to keep a low profile during the first 90 days of the season.

"One of our late-season strategies is to have trail cameras out on some of our food plots that we know the deer are hitting.

Checking those cameras can tell us a lot about which bucks are feeding in certain fields. If you've done your homework and you already have a pretty good idea about the number of mature bucks you have on your farm, you should know most of these bucks from their photos.

"By this time of the year, however, you might not even know which of your oldest bucks are still alive (after gun or shotgun season), so those trail camera photos can be invaluable in giving you that information. Trail-camera photos might also identify new bucks on your late-season food plots that you've never seen before. Obviously, these bucks have traveled to your farm because of the good food you have to offer.

"That's where our standing corn really makes a huge difference. We often go in and mow down several rows of corn and put up a ground blind just inside the standing stalks. You can get in and get out quietly and be right there where the deer are feeding. But again, getting an opportunity to shoot a mature buck during late season really boils down to what you've been doing the previous three months.

"Did you and your friends beat the place up so badly that the deer aren't moving until midnight because they've been so totally spooked? Or did you do your best to keep somewhat of a low profile so that the deer haven't been scared to death? If so, your chances of seeing a good buck during late season will be greatly enhanced.

"Except for the really cold temperatures, late-season hunting strategy is pretty much the same as it is all year. The one exception might be that afternoon hunting is probably a lot more productive than early-morning hunting. If you plan to hunt in the morning, you have to get to your stand without spooking any deer. That can be a real challenge because not only do you have deer feeding out in the field, you might have some bedding along the edges as well.

"On the other hand, when you hunt the afternoons, you can get to your stand early and get settled in — say around 1:30 p.m. or so — before the deer start coming out to feed. As the afternoon progresses, you'll see the 1½-year-old bucks come out with the does. Then the 2½-year-olds and the 3½-year-olds start coming out. Usually, the old boys don't come out until 30 minutes or less before dark. Sometimes, it'll be the last five minutes before dark. Often they'll stand just inside the trees for an hour or more, watching the field and making sure everything is just right before they'll step out into the open.

> It stands to reason that by the time the late season arrives in late December, the deer on your place probably know they are being hunted.

"I normally like to put up a couple of cameras in the corn where we'll be hunting to see what is coming out. As I'll mention in an upcoming chapter, I always have cameras set up on the edges of fields, but when we hunt in the corn, I'll sometimes tie several corn stalks together and attach a camera to them near my ground blind. Other times, I might use a stake to set the camera on. The photos we get tell us how many mature bucks are coming into the corn and the exact times they are feeding.

"In the late season, weather conditions also make a huge difference in your hunting success. Obviously if it's warm outside, the deer might stop moving altogether and lay down on you. Even if it isn't super cold, though, I've learned that you're always going to have good deer movement two days before a front moves in and two days after. The day before a front moves in might not necessarily be that good. Ideally, however, we always have our best days on cold, clear high-pressure days. But even when you have a string of days like that, and a weather front suddenly moves in where it might be cloudy or snowy, the deer are always going to be on their feet early two days before that front hits.

> If deer find an area they like that offers them safety and a good food supply, they'll relocate and stay. That's why it's so important to make your property the only show in town in the late season.

"The opposite conditions are even better. During times of high humidity and low pressure with a lot of cloud cover, you might be seeing a few deer, but ultimately when you get that weather change that turns to cold and clear, you can just about bet that you're going to see a ton of deer, especially bucks. The weather is such a big deal for us during late season. It's important any time during the season, but in the late season especially, everything always depends on those weather changes. If you're going to shoot a big buck during the later season, you can just about set your clock to those critical conditions.

"Like I've said many times before, deer are creatures of habit, and they get conditioned to feed in certain areas. If they find an area they like that offers them safety and a good food supply, they'll relocate and stay. That's why it's so important to make your property the only show in town in the late season.

"Because this is the one time of year when we also hunt with muzzleloaders, we don't have to get as close as we do with archery gear. Hunting out of pop-up ground blinds definitely help shield you from the wind and the elements. And when the temperature is hovering around zero, anything you can do to be protected from the wind makes sitting out there all afternoon a lot more bearable.

"Another great product that we absolutely love are heated boots made by Columbia that come with rechargeable batteries. I've never seen anything like it for keeping your feet warm. Tiffany can be out in below-zero temperatures, and they'll last up to eight hours on the lowest setting, six hours on medium and four on high. When it's extremely cold, Tiffany also uses heat pads that she tapes to various parts of her body. With the help of those heat pads, she usually manages to stay pretty warm.

"While bow-hunting, I always wear thin gloves, and I use a hand muff. I also wear heated boots f it's really cold. There are certainly times that I use heat pads for my hands, especially when it's below zero. With my Under Armour base layers and heavier fleece jacket, I can usually sit out in anything.

"It really comes down to your hands and feet. If you can keep your hands and feet warm, you've won half the battle. We sometimes use propane heaters in ground blinds or box blinds in extremely bad weather, but I really don't use them that much because they fog up the windows so bad in the box blinds. I don't worry about the scent of a propane heater that much because I'm always hunting the wind anyway, but they do cause other problems. If you're in one of the box blinds, it's nice because you don't have to have your hands in a muff, and they serve as a good windbreak, just like ground blinds do."

"Because we're out there nearly every day of the season, we more or less build up to the really cold weather and get acclimated to it as the season progresses," Tiffany said. "By the time extremely cold weather arrives in late season, we've gotten used to the colder temperatures. I know what I can put on when it's 30 degrees outside, and I know what I can wear when it's a lot colder."

CHAPTER 11

THE IMPORTANCE OF SHED HUNTING

Everyone knows there is a magical quality about shed antlers. Not only is each found shed antler a unique treasure, but knowing the buck that shed that antler is still out there somewhere only adds to the mystery and magic. Like so many other facets of their deer hunting world, shed hunting is a vital part of the overall Lakosky management program.

And even though it's a lot of hard work, shed hunting is also fun and exciting. During late Winter 2011, Lee picked up more than 300 shed antlers on the various farms he hunts. That total represented several long weeks of searching from daylight to dark. Lee and Tiffany; Tiffany's mom, Linda; and the latest edition to their family — Tank, a beautiful black Lab that's a

Sheds are very important to Lee and Tiffany because of the information they reveal about specific deer. Here, Lee poses with a massive 4-by-4 he named the Big Brow Tine Buck.

fanatical shed antler dog — love to get back in the woods in late winter to search for sheds. Each shed antler is a unique piece of history and a clue as to a buck's habits and secrets. And especially to Lee, each shed is a true work of art.

Lee has several thousand shed antlers of all sizes and shapes at his house, accumulated during the past six or seven hunting seasons in Iowa. Some are singles, and some are matched sets. Amazingly, you can grab almost any antler out of any pile, and Lee can tell you where and when it was found and something about the buck that carried it. To Lee and Tiffany, finding the antlers from the bucks they hunt is a much anticipated yearly activity. It's also extremely important because of the information that sheds provide.

"Sheds tell you a lot about a buck's life-style," Lee said. "They give you hints as to where he might be bedding, the trails he is using on a regular basis and where he is feeding. When you combine that information with the other sign in the woods you find in late winter — like scrapes, rubs and tracks — it all goes together like the pieces of a huge puzzle to help you learn everything you can about that deer. That information can give you a lot of clues about how to hunt him.

"If you happen to have several antlers from the same buck dropped in consecutive years, you can see how well a buck is progressing each year and how many inches he has added on. In the case of a very old buck, you can see how much he might be going downhill. In some cases, a buck might get to a certain point and never get beyond it. Say he's a genetic 140-inch 10-pointer, and he'll never grow a rack beyond that size. The sheds you find from him each year will tell you that he's never going to be a 160.

"If you don't know a buck's exact age, his sheds can give you a good idea of how old he is. The sheds of a young buck are fairly easy to age. With older bucks, it's a little more difficult, but at least you have a good idea of whether he's 4½ or a real old-timer of 7½.

"Sheds also give you a buck's exact score. Trail-camera photos can sometimes distort a deer's rack, and it might actually be larger or smaller than you think it is. Sometimes, you might only get one or two photos of a buck that don't show the entire rack clearly and distinctly. Or the angle of the photo might be bad, and you can't see all of the points a buck has, especially if he has several burr points or flyers coming off the back of his beam. But when you get that antler in your hand, there is no question about how long the main beam is, how long the tines are and the number of odd points.

"After you find a buck's sheds, if you see him the next year standing in a field or start getting new trail-camera pictures of him, you'll have a much better idea of how big he is and what his new rack will score. You'll know what kind of jump he's made from one year to the next. That information can mean a lot in deciding whether you want to hunt him when the season opens.

"I take a picture of every shed antler I find before I pick it up. That way, I have a permanent record of where it was found. Was it found on a grassy hillside near a food plot where that buck had been bedded down chewing his cud during the night? Was it found on a trail in the timber not far from that buck's bedding area? Was it found in the snow near a cedar thicket where that buck was toughing out a brutal winter storm? All of these locations can give you valuable hints about where that buck is spending his time.

A Method to Lee's Madness

"Whenever I'm shed hunting in late winter, I never walk a large section of the farm I'm on at one time. Instead, I always break down each part of that farm into small sections or grids. For example, if I plan to search a 20-acre section of timber, I'll only walk about half of it at one time. Then I'll come back a few days later and do the other half. That way, if I happen to disturb some deer in one section, they'll simply move over to the other section without leaving the property.

"After I do a few sections of one farm in the morning, I'll typically head over to another farm and do the same thing there in the afternoon. That way I'm not putting too much pressure on any one spot. I'll come back to the first farm a week or so later and hit the section that I missed the first time. I'll continue to do that until I've covered the entire farm. Usually I do it in quarters or sixths so I never run deer completely off of the farm where they live.

"When snow is on the ground, you can see all of the bedding areas in the timber and where the main trails are located that lead in and out of those areas. So you are actually scouting the woods for next season while you are looking for sheds.

"Interestingly enough, if it's been a really cold winter with lots of snow previous to the time that most bucks start shedding their antlers, we'll find most of our antlers on the ridges closest to the food plots, and they'll be fairly easy to find. That makes sense, because the deer never go far from the food source when the weather is miserable. If the weather has been unusually

mild in January and February, however, the sheds will always be farther away and harder to find.

"It's nice to have all those sheds because you know what you've got in the way of deer. If you're really watching your farm carefully, you should already know about most of the big deer living on it. But in late season, if you have plenty of food available, you might also get some big bucks from other areas coming in and staying, at least until the worst of the cold weather is gone.

"And if you find the sheds from one of these bucks, at least you know he's close by some-where. You know he's not far. If he's not living on your farm year-round, the challenge will be to entice him to do so by giving him all the food he can eat and good protective cover to hide in where he feels totally unpressured.

"Even if he leaves the property during summer and the early part of the season (like Gnarles Barkley; see Chapter 5) he'll remember where those doe bedding areas were located and where that good food was available in late season. He might come back during the rut or later on after the rut. And he might well be one of those older bucks that got moved off the property several years earlier by one of the younger, more aggressive bucks. Even if you don't see him for two or three years, he might simply show up one day. And his sheds will tell you how big he has gotten.

"Having a collection of shed antlers that you've acquired through a period of time also shows you what the potential is on your farm from year to year. You learn exactly what each age-class of bucks is capable of growing each year and what you should expect from your 2½-year-olds, your 3½-year-olds and so on. And with a good year-round nutritional program in place that gives your deer all the food they need, you'll also be able to see what kind of increase you're getting in antler mass as a result of that added nutrition.

Tank the black Labrador became a part of Lee and Tiffany's family in 2010 and is quickly turning into a first-class shed dog.

"As mentioned, when we first moved to Iowa, I was surprised at how many sheds we found in high grass, old fields where cattle once grazed or low brushy areas that offered good cover. Big bucks like to bed in CRP fields or grassy areas during extremely cold weather because high grass offers good cover and protection from the wind. It also offers warmth from the sun on cold winter days. Through the years, we've found a large number of big sheds in these areas. In fact, we find very few sheds out in our food plots.

"Why? Because mature bucks spend a relatively brief amount of time in any given food plot during a 24-hour period. Instead, we find a lot more sheds in the grassy hillsides overlooking the food plots. That big buck might feed for only 20 minutes or so. Then he'll go and bed down on the hillside next to the food plot and chew his cud for two hours or longer in the pre-dawn darkness.

"Further, we never find as many sheds in the timber as we do on the more open edges. And that's a good thing, because squirrels and other rodents don't spend much time out in those more open areas. There are too many hawks and other predators searching those open areas for prey.

A Shed Dog Named Tank

"During Summer 2010, Tiffany and I got a black Lab puppy that had been trained to find shed antlers. He was also trained to retrieve ducks and pheasants. We named him Tank, and he immediately became a special member of the family. The next winter, when he was 8 months old, I took Tank shed hunting with me. It was his first official shed season.

"Just like with pheasant hunting or any other kind of bird hunting, dogs are fun to watch and fun to be with. Tank is no different. He is obsessed with antlers, and while we were out on each farm, he stayed close and worked hard. I didn't allow him to run around in the timber because I didn't want to spook any deer. He still has a lot to learn, but I think he'll be a first-class shed dog in another year or so.

"As mentioned, we found more than 300 sheds during late Winter 2011. I never picked up a single one of them. Instead,

In April 2011, Tank won the junior and amateur titles at the National Shed Dog Championships in Northfield, Minn.

I let Tank pick up every single antler. He found a few on his own — mostly by scent instead of sight — but in most instances, I saw them first and directed him to them. When he starts using his eyes instead of his nose, I think he'll find a lot more sheds.

"Sheds have a definite scent, especially newer sheds. I watched Tank run right past several older sheds that had been out there for at least a year. I think dogs find more sheds visually than they do by using their noses. Their eyes are trained to look for that white object out there. Dog trainers like Tank's trainer, Tom Dokken, often use white paper attached to a shed for this purpose.

"In April 2011, Tom asked us if we'd take Tank up to the National Shed Dog Championships that he was putting on in Northfield, Minn., sponsored by the North American Shed Hunting Dog Association. We were happy to comply because we wanted to see what Tank could do. Amazingly, as an 8-month-old Lab, he won two out of three of his divisions. He won the junior and amateur titles, and he missed winning the third division, the pro division, by only a couple of seconds. It was won by an 8-year-old dog that had many years of experience. Tiffany and I were so proud of Tank. He really made us look good.

"Shed hunting is a passion in itself, and I spend a lot of time looking for antlers. There are probably other things on the farm that I could be doing that would be a lot more important, but Tiffany and I love getting out in the woods to look for sheds. In addition to Tiffany's mom, who often goes out with us, one or two of my friends from Minnesota usually come down each season. In 2011, my good friend Lee Murphy came down and spent a few days with us. He picked up more than 20 sheds.

"And with the addition of a good shed dog like Tank, we've added another dimension to our shed hunting pursuits. Tiffany and I really enjoyed getting out with him as well. But even if you don't have an antler dog, just being out there at that time of year is fun and educational. You can learn so much about what

THE IMPORTANCE OF SHED HUNTING

your deer are doing in late season. And by studying the deer sign, which is so easy to see when the woods are so open, you'll know where to hunt and where to place your stands for the upcoming hunting season."

215

CHAPTER 12

CHOOSE YOUR STAND SITES CAREFULLY

To a hunter, a tree stand is an invaluable piece of equipment. It's really a conduit that directly connects him with the world of his quarry. In some ways, a tree stand can be a hunter's life's blood. And when the quarry is a 5½-year-old white-tailed buck, you need every advantage you can get, because the challenge is never easy. More deer are probably killed from tree stands than by any other method of hunting, especially among bow-hunters. Like Lee said, if you attempt to stalk into the timber where big bucks commonly bed, your chances of getting close enough for a successful bow shot are probably one in 100. That's why tree stands and their precise placement are vitally important to your success.

"If you do your homework during shed season, you'll know where all the big scrapes and rubs are located in the woods," Lee said. "A lot of times, those scrapes will be in the same place, and those big 4- to 6-inch rubs will be hit year after year. You might not know exactly which bucks are making them, but you know that you have some big, mature bucks on your property.

"During shed season, if I see any deer sign that looks particularly good, like a string of large scrapes or a rub line next to a cedar swamp, I'll probably put up a stand, if I don't already have one up in the area. After that stand is in place, I usually won't go back in there until the rut. Then I'll find out if those scrapes and rubs are still being used by the same buck. Usually they are. During hunting season, I don't ever walk around trying to find out what the deer are doing. If I've done my homework properly back during late winter, I should already know.

"I probably set up 90 percent of my new stands during shed season. I would never do it at any other time of year if I had an unlimited amount of time. During Spring 2011, I put up around 20 new stands on several new pieces of property that we recently acquired. But I still failed to get stands up in another five to 10 locations because I simply didn't have the time. I did pick out the trees I planned to use, and I went back in early summer and finished the job. That was still four months before archery season.

"If you get in there during January or February, everything looks the same as it does during hunting season. There are no leaves on the trees, you can see all the trails, and you can see all the rubs and scrapes. You don't ever want to go out in the middle of August to put up a stand when it's buggy and hot. What's more, the leaves are so thick at that time of year you can't possibly know what those woods are going to look like in November when the trees are bare.

"In August, you have no way of knowing what the deer will be doing a few months later during hunting season. If you put up a stand in late summer, you might get up there in November when the leaves are down and discover that you stand out like a sore thumb. Or you might discover that you have limbs in your way or other objects in your shooting lane because you had no way of knowing what things looked like when the leaves were down.

"I always try to use any cover to my advantage so that I won't stand out or be sky-lighted in a tree. But if I happen to hang a stand in a tree that has no cover around it, I'll put up several bunches of fake leaves around it at the time I hang it. The leaf systems I use come on bendable wires that can be shaped to camouflage the outline of the stand.

"Granted, in late winter when the real leaves are gone, those fake leaf systems sometimes look like a big blob up in that tree to a live deer, but that's what you want. By the next fall, the deer are used to seeing that blob, and when you get up in that stand, you're just another part of that blob the deer are already used to seeing. So they seldom pay any attention to it any more after all that time.

"When it comes to hunting big deer, there are so many details that come into play to be successful. You might get by with skipping one or two of them, but if you really want to be consistent, you'd better pay attention to even the tiniest of details. And a lot of it comes down to doing your homework during the off-season.

Safety First — Always

"Even though I hang most of my new stands during shed season, I rarely take down any old stands. If they're in a good spot, they usually remain in place for several years. However, I check all of my older stands on each farm while I'm out shed hunting to make sure they're safe and in good working order. I always make sure the platforms are propped up against the tree during the months they are not in use. That takes the pressure off the straps while the tree is growing.

"Because we always hunt with a cameraman, we always have two stands set up in any given location. The camera stand is usually just above and to the right of the hunter's stand. Before we hunt any of our old stands in fall, Tiffany and I always go out and check the straps and the lifeline ropes. We make sure they are safe and secure before we hunt them, or before any of our guests come to hunt later on.

"Whenever we're out shed hunting in late winter, I always keep — in the truck — a large backpack full of new straps, safety ropes, saws, snippers and anything else we might need to work on our stands. Nearly all of the stands we use are Ameristep Outfitters, and I keep boxes of extra straps and spare parts on hand at home. Normally, we replace all of the straps on each stand every two to three years. Because the trees grow every year, we make a point of replacing all old straps before they get so tight against the tree that you can't get them off.

"We are extremely safety conscious, and we have lifeline ropes attached to all of the stands we hunt. We use lifeline ropes from Hunter Safety Systems, and sometimes the ropes get chewed by squirrels or get stiff from exposure to the weather, so we replace them as needed. Instead of using screw-in tree steps, we always use strap-on climbers or strap-on ladder sections to get up to all of our hanging stands. And in a few rare instances, we have a couple of regular ladder stands out in the woods.

"New stands that have been out in the woods for a year or less seldom require any maintenance, but stands that have been out for several years often do, and those are the ones we check very carefully. We have some stands that have never been hunted for one reason or another. And because things might change on certain farms from year to year, we have some stands that haven't been hunted in several years. But you never know when you might need to use one of them.

> Even though I hang most of my new stands during shed season, I rarely take down any old stands. If they're in a good spot, they usually remain in place for several years.

Choosing the Right Tree

"Whenever I'm hanging a stand, I always look for trees with good cover. Cedars are one of my favorites but they're not always available in a lot of areas. If they are, you can cut some limbs away and tuck your stand right into the branches and be very well hidden. Cedars are also great for ground blinds because you can tuck the blind right in under those limbs and just about disappear. Certain types of oak trees hold their leaves well into late season, and whenever I'm out shed hunting in March, I always look for those oaks that still have their leaves.

"None of our stands are exceptionally high; usually 18 to 25 feet depending on the tree. We have a couple that are higher because they are on field edges that slope down and away from the field, and you have to go up about 10 feet before you get to the field level. We have a couple that are around 30 feet high because they are on the sides of hills, and you don't want to look over at the hill behind you and have a deer staring at you face to face. I don't like getting any stand too high because it affects the shot angle, and if you get too high, it could affect your ability to get both lungs.

"Generally, I'd rather use a bad tree in a perfect spot rather than a good tree in a bad spot. We use the leaf systems on some of our stands, as mentioned, to help hide them and make them blend in with their surroundings. It's especially tough when you're in a stand at the top of a hill, because the deer are usually walking uphill and looking up as they are walking, and it's very easy for them to see your silhouette and pick you off. I always try to avoid being at the very top of a hill, but sometimes you can't help it. If we can't find a tree that has a lot of branches or a lot of cover behind it, we'll use the leaf system.

"If I were hunting by myself, I'd always put my stand on the back side of a tree and shoot around it. But because I always hunt with a cameraman, I can't do that. So I try to figure out which way the deer will come from and place my stand in such a position so that I'll be standing flat up against the trunk of the tree. That helps break up my outline, but the cameraman is always off to one side, so he's a little more visible. That makes it a lot tougher, because a camera stand has to have plenty of open space for filming. It always helps to pick a tree that has some sort of cover behind it.

Hang 'Em Right

"When I was younger, I used to put up all of my stands in August like most other hunters I knew at the time. But I learned a long time ago that it's so much better to do it late winter when the woods are open. Usually, Tiffany and I put up stands together. Sometimes, one of our cameramen will be with us, and we'll work together as a three-person team. It's always a production. We have gotten a stand up in 20 or 30 minutes, but to do it right, it usually takes us about an hour per stand.

"We try to do everything the right way the first time so that we never have to go back and do it again. After we're finished, that stand is ready to hunt. We always put up easy hangers, hooks for your bow and backpack, and a safety rope at each stand site. When we're done, that stand has everything it needs to be safe, secure and productive.

"I have two pole saws — one that is gas-powered — that telescope out to 20 feet, and I make sure that all of the shooting lanes are trimmed out properly and that no branches are in the way to interfere with a bow shot. Sometimes, I'll take a chain saw, cut down several trees and place them in a ditch or along the trail so any approaching deer will have to move around them in a way that will offer a good broadside shot from the stand.

Away-From-Home Tree-Stand Tactics

"Whenever we're hunting away from home, our tree-stand strategies are pretty much the same as they are in Iowa. For example, we usually go to Alberta every September to hunt early-season velvet whitetails. The guide we hunt with, Larry Joliffe of Northern Wilderness Outfitters, is always great about letting us more or less do our own thing as far as hanging stands and hunting goes.

"But the fact is, we haven't been on that property for an entire year. And even though we're familiar with it, we obviously haven't been able to do our homework. Larry always tells us everything he knows about deer movement and specific deer he has seen in the area we'll be hunting, but I still like to revert to the way I always hunt at home.

"For starters, we always stay out of the timber to begin with. On the first day of the hunt, Tiffany and I usually hang our stands on the outside edges of fields, just as we would if we were hunting a new area at home. Then we watch for does

> We try to do everything the right way the first time so that we never have to go back and do it again. After we're finished, that stand is ready to hunt.

Lee would rather hang a stand at a bad tree in a perfect spot instead of a great tree in a bad spot.

coming out and watch to see what the deer are doing. As their movement patterns begin to unfold, we slowly start to work our way from the outside edges into the timber on a gradual basis. But you never want to pop right into the timber the first time out.

"We always concentrate on getting in and out of our stands without disturbing any deer, just as we do at home. We tend to do more observing the first few times out than actual hunting so that we can try to learn what is going on around us. If a nice buck comes out, that's great, but more than anything else, it's important to know what the deer are doing.

"We want to learn things like which fields the bucks are coming into and which trails they are using to get in and out. Again, the outfitter can often tell you things like that so you don't necessarily have to start from scratch. Back when I first started hunting seriously for big whitetails, that's the way I always did it because it was the only thing I knew to do.

"I would start on the field edges and find out which trails the bucks were coming out of near inside corners. Then, if I saw one or more good bucks coming into the field, I would go back the next afternoon and put up a stand over on the side where I saw those deer. But never would I go busting into the timber right off the bat. And that's the way I've always done things ever since. That strategy has worked well for me through the years. No matter where Tiffany and I are hunting, at home or away from home, that's the way we like to do it.

Patience Is Golden

"I think the biggest single factor in placing a stand on any property is being patient and watching the deer carefully so you know where your stand needs to be set up. Take the farm where I shot Gnarles Barkley, for example. We've had that farm now for four years. And Winter 2011 was actually the first time in four years that I felt comfortable enough to put up two stands in the timber. It took that long for me to learn the property well enough to make the decision to finally do it.

"I actually had put one other stand in the timber two years earlier near the spot where I found one of Gnarles' sheds. But that stand was set up at the end of a little four-wheeler road that led down into the timber. And

even though it had been in there for a while, I never really liked hunting that spot because you had to cross a small clover field to get into the woods, and I always felt like I was bumping a deer or two whenever I went in there. It just never felt right.

"I did hunt it a couple of times in the mornings during the 2010 season after I'd seen a big 6-by-6 in there. Later in the season, my good friend Greg Ritz actually shot that deer from the same stand the first time he ever went in there. The buck was probably a 4½- or 5½-year-old deer, and he scored in the 150s.

So in early 2011, after shed hunting season was finished, I finally felt confident enough to go in there and set up two more stands back in the timber. Every other stand we've had on that farm has been on a field edge or just inside the woods only a few yards. Only time will tell if my decision was a smart one.

"On most of the farms we hunt that are around 300 to 400 acres, we'll usually have three to four mature bucks living on that farm. It's funny how they all have their own little spot or core area where the other mature bucks seldom or never go. You'll see one buck in one spot all the time, and then if you move down to another section of the farm, you'll see a different buck in that section.

"We have a buck called Skyscraper on the farm where I shot Gnarles, which I've mentioned before. You'll see trail camera pictures of him often in the middle field and the southern field but never up on the northern end of the property. After two years of getting dozens and dozens of photos of him, we've never seen him up in the northern field. On the other hand, the big 9-pointer that I shot on that same farm in 2010 was always seen in the middle field and to the north but never in the south.

"I decided to hunt him in 2010, and I moved several stands around in the edge of the timber along the northern field where we had been seeing him most of the time. I hunted one stand in particular morning and night for two days in a row — a total of four sits. And wouldn't you know it? During each one of those sits, we always saw him on the other side of the field. In truth, he seemed to be all over the place — except where I was set up.

"I noticed that he was coming out of the woods most often in one particular spot on the other side of the field from where my stand was set up, so I went back during the middle of the day and moved my stand closer to that spot. I actually had him right underneath me the first afternoon that I hunted the new location, but it was so late we didn't have enough camera light for filming. So we went back the next morning, and he came right by me again. That time I was able to put an arrow in him. That stand was just slightly inside the timber.

"When it's necessary, we occasionally hunt on the fly. The hunt for that deer really came about through patience and observation. We saw him several times and tried to get some stands in the area where he was coming out of the timber.

"One day in October during that season when it was unusually warm, we had a couple of friends visiting for a few days — Tom Roles and his wife, Kari, from Minnesota. Because it was so warm, we got together and said, 'You know, let's don't even hunt this afternoon. Instead, let's watch a couple of fields to see what the deer are doing.' So, from a distance, we went and

watched the same field where I later hunted the big 9-pointer. We saw him come out of the woods and into the field from one particular corner.

"Because we didn't have a stand in that spot, Tiffany and I went out the next afternoon and put one up in that corner. As things turned out, the 9-pointer never made an appearance that evening. But a 160-inch-plus 8-pointer came out very close to my stand, and I ended up shooting him. It was fairly early in the evening when I shot him, and the 9-pointer might well have come out a little closer to dark if I hadn't shot the big 8. Later in the season, I ended up shooting the big 9, too. Both of those deer were what we considered to be management bucks, but they were mature animals, and I was very happy to shoot them.

"So a lot of times, you base your hunting strategy on what you see. If you don't get it right the first time, you do something different and try again. And sometimes it pays to take a little time off and go watch the area you're hunting for an afternoon instead of actually hunting from a stand. In that case, it certainly paid off for me.

"It's easy to get in the mode of, 'I can't kill one if I'm not in my tree hunting.' But if you take a night off and go check several different fields from a distance to see what the deer are doing, you might discover something very important that you didn't know. I've done that several times during the past few seasons, and it's always benefited me greatly."

Used correctly, ground blinds can be a great weapon in your deer hunting arsenal.

CHAPTER 13

THE IMPORTANCE OF TRAIL CAMERAS

G one are those unforgettable days when you had to take several rolls of film from your trail cameras to Wal-Mart or a one-hour photo lab and waited impatiently while that film was being developed. Then you tore open the package to see what antlered treasures might be revealed inside. You flipped through 15 or 20 shots, and there it was, the picture you were hoping to see: Mr. Big in his glory.

In addition to the time involved and the cost of film, processing and batteries, those early trail cameras were often unpredictable at best. But the cost didn't matter. You would have done anything for a picture of that big buck on your farm. Now that has changed, and technology is light years ahead of where it used to be.

22/2008   4:25 PM

Keeping track of thousands of digital images requires a lot of work.

"I keep my trail cameras out pretty much year-round," Lee said. "I pull some at certain times of the year, but there are always several cameras out on each of our farms. We get thousands of trail-camera photos each year, and I spend a lot of time studying them. They can tell you so much about the deer on your farm. At peak times, I probably have 70 to 80 cameras out on all of the various farms we hunt. But even during slower times, I'll have at least a dozen or more cameras operating all the time.

"We use our cameras for various functions at different times of the year. From June until Jan. 10, when hunting season closes, we're obviously trying to keep tabs on certain bucks in certain areas. We're looking for specific deer that are on the hit list. But we're also looking at other younger bucks and watching their progress.

"After the season closes, we look for specific bucks in January and February to see if they made it through the season. This is also the time of year when new bucks might show up on one of our farms, so we watch them very carefully and try to learn as much about them as we can. The more we can learn about them, the better our chances to keep them on our property.

"As soon as the bucks start to shed their antlers, our cameras are invaluable because the photos tell us when certain bucks have dropped their antlers. Because I don't like to go into the timber any more than necessary — even during shed season — as soon as a buck I am watching drops his antlers, I can go right in and look for his antlers without wasting a lot of time. And the photos give me a good idea of where to look.

"In the case of a large 5½- or 6½-year-old buck that we might be hunting, or even in the case of younger 4½-year-olds that we plan to target in a year or so, knowing exactly when those bucks have shed is so important, because you want to get in there and find their antlers before they get chewed up by squirrels. And even though it's never been a serious problem on any of our farms, you always run the risk of having trespassers slip in and steal some of your sheds. So it's important to get in there to look for specific sheds as quickly as possible. Our cameras tell us when and where to do that.

"Trail cameras help us narrow down specific areas to search for targeted sheds, because they tell us where those particular bucks have been feeding, which fields they've been using or where their sheds are likely to be in the nearby timber. Of course, we don't always find every shed from every big buck in the timber. We often find them along the edges of food plots, in grassy fields near food plots and in CRP fields. In fact, those places are where I usually look first. Then, if I don't find the sheds I'm looking for, I'll go into the timber.

"Generally, most of our bucks shed their antlers any time from early January through late March, depending on a lot of factors. But our cameras have taught us that specific bucks drop their antlers at almost the same time every year. That is, if a certain buck drops his antlers on Feb. 12 one year, he'll more than likely drop them on almost the same date the next year. From previous photos, I know to start looking for that buck's antlers at about that time.

"Usually I start going into the timber around Feb. 20 to look for sheds. Before that, I'll hit the fields and open edges around food plots in the middle of the afternoon while the bucks are bedded back in the timber. From the hundreds of photos that we get each year, we know that several of our deer don't shed their antlers until April 1.

"After shed season is finished in April and May, we continue to watch all of the bucks we know on each farm through their growing collection of photos. We also use our cameras to monitor turkey activity so we know where all the big gobblers are when spring turkey season starts. When turkey season opens, our trail photos often tell us where the gobblers are strutting and where most of the turkeys are hanging out.

"In June, as bucks are growing their new antlers, we repeat our yearly cycle by watching them and monitoring their new growth. As soon the antlers start sprouting up and branching out on some of our bucks in early May, it's amazing how easy it is for me to identify those bucks by the way their antlers are shaped.

> We use our cameras for various functions at different times of the year.

A Storehouse of Knowledge

"I always place my cameras on field edges or along roads in the woods where I can get to them fairly easily. I never place them in the timber where I would risk spooking deer if I went in to check the cards. It makes sense to put cameras along the field edges near food plots anyway. That's where the deer tend to congregate the most at night and during the daytime (early morning and late afternoon), and that's where we are going to get pictures of the largest numbers of deer.

10/19/07 1:34 AM

10/28/07 12:04 AM

Cuddeback

"Often, when I'm out fertilizing or mowing on the tractor on a particular farm, I'll drop by a camera location during the middle of the afternoon to change out the cards. The deer are so used to seeing the tractor that it's never alarming to them. Or if I'm driving into or out of an area on my Bad Boy Buggy while hunting, I'll quietly swing by and switch out the card in any camera that might be nearby. As always, my goal is to check the cameras without spooking any deer. I try to check my cameras every three or four days because I certainly don't want to miss out on that giant buck that suddenly makes an appearance.

8/30/08 12:46 AM

"I never use cameras to try to kill deer. I use them to study the deer and take an inventory of what we've got on each farm. I want to know what's out there. From trail photos, we can tell the age of certain bucks, which ones are shooters and how much they've grown since the previous season. We can tell which fields certain bucks are hanging out in the most, which trails they are using and what time of day they are coming out to feed.

"I attach my cameras to all sorts of things: trees, fence posts and several commercial products, such as Trail Pods, which are made for holding cameras. When I'm cutting corn and hunting in it (see Chapter 13), I want to know which bucks are feeding in it. But obviously, there are no trees out in the middle of the corn-fields where I can attach cameras. I used to solve that problem by tying four or five corn stalks together and attaching a camera to the top of the bunch. However, I soon found that deer would come up and nuzzle them out of curios-ity and often knock them over. Or sometimes, raccoons would climb the stalks and knock the cameras sideways. So I started using tripods and steel posts instead. Typically, I'll set them up one row inside the standing corn and knock the tops off of the stalks in front of the camera. That strategy has worked well for me.

"Trail cameras give us so much good informa-tion about our deer. One of the most important bits of informa-tion on each photo is the time of day — or night — it was taken. Say we get several early-season photos of a big buck coming out

> We can tell which fields certain bucks are hanging out in the most, which trails they are using and what time of day they are coming out to feed.

2007-10-26 10:51:33 PM M 2/3

RECONYX

LAKOSKY

Lee and Tiffany enjoy getting trail camera pictures of bucks they've seen during previous seasons.

to feed at 5:30 p.m. during a three- or four-day period. Or maybe we'll get three or four photos of one of the 5½-year-old bucks on our hit list that were taken in the same spot at 7:30 a.m. Armed with that kind of information, you can plan your hunting strategy accordingly.

"Our photos also tell us so much about deer behavior. We can see which bucks are aggressive, which are not and which ones are dominant. On several occasions during the rut, we've gotten pictures of a hot doe in one of our food plots with a big buck right behind her. In a situation like that, you know that buck is apt to be with that doe for at least four days, and there's a good chance both of them will hang around the same area during that time. So, thanks to that trail camera photo, you know you'd better get in there while the iron is hot and do something about it. Most of our mature bucks will take a hot doe to a secluded CRP field or some other isolated spot, as mentioned in other chapters, but occasionally they'll hang out in a food plot. We've seen it happen more than once.

"Because most of our cameras are set up around food sources and close to woods roads, I'm able to check them on a regular basis. If I'm not working on the tractor on a certain farm, I might jump in the truck during the middle of the day and run out and change cards.

"It's kind of neat seeing those deer that you recognize from previous seasons — even early in the season. Then you can follow their antler growth throughout summer by monitoring your trail-camera photos. And if you do get a chance to shoot one of these bucks later when hunting season opens, it's nice to have pictures of the deer in velvet, and it's nice to have a record of his antler-growth period.

"Many of our bucks have come pretty far along with their antler growth by early June, when I'm still out planting on the tractor. The big 9-pointer I shot in 2010 was nearly fully formed by the middle of June. Some bucks start growing their antlers a lot sooner than others. Those that tend to grow earlier in the season also tend to shed earlier the next winter. Those that shed late usually get a later start on growing. That's the kind of information that makes our trail cameras invaluable to us.

"Although it hasn't been a big problem for us in the past, as mentioned, we use cameras to photograph and discourage trespassers. Naturally if a trespasser is going to come in, he'll look for sheds in the same places that we do. So I try to make sure that some of my cameras are well hidden on field edges and along field roads. And believe it or not, we actually have gotten photos of trespassers on several of our farms.

"One in particular was caught red-handed on camera with several sheds in his possession. We have no-trespassing signs posted at all of our gates and along many of our boundaries. The signs at the gates read, 'Private property, do not trespass, monitored by hidden video. If you need access, please call this number.' Most people respect our property rights and call and ask for permission if they need to get on the property for any legitimate reason.

Flash Cameras Vs. Infrared Cameras

"As mentioned, we have some live cameras set up on our home farm, and I've often used them to see how deer react to infra-red cameras versus flash cameras. So many people think that the deer, especially big bucks, are going to leave the country when a camera flashes in their face. But from what I've seen with our deer in Iowa, they don't react much differently to a flash than they do to infrared, even if that flash is right in their face. According to my experience, they react pretty much the same way to both cameras, so I don't have a problem using flash cameras to inventory our deer.

"Basically, my goal is to get good, clean pictures of our deer, and I want to be able to see every point clearly and distinctly. If they've got any stickers or anything like that, I want to be able to see those as well. With infrared cameras, the picture is often blurred if the deer happens to move. Also, the pictures often have a greenish hue, and they sometimes appear to be very fuzzy. So I prefer to use flash cameras because of the clarity of the photos I get.

"I will admit that if I put a flash camera over a scrape on the edge of a field, I might get one or two pictures of a mature buck, but I seldom get another picture of him in that same spot again, because he apparently remembers that flash. But like I said, I watch those bucks all the time with my live cameras, and they're still coming into the fields where those flash cameras are set up. They don't leave the area. They simply move down the edge of the field 20 yards or so to another scrape because they don't want that flash going off in their face again.

"So I've found that the flash really doesn't bother them that much, and it certainly doesn't keep them away or make them go some place else like some people seem to think. Plus we've had numerous bucks that really don't seem to be concerned about the flash at all. Those are usually the bucks that have been living on that particular farm for two or three years, and they've gotten used to it. They'll stand out there all summer, night after night, with those flashes popping in their faces, and it doesn't seem to bother them one bit. Sometimes, I'll get 50 pictures of the same buck in one night with that flash popping right in his face.

"But some deer do care, especially the newer deer that have not lived on that farm their entire lives. They're all different, and they're all individuals. One thing I've learned with my infrared cameras is that if I set them up high — say six feet or so off the ground — and point them down at a scrape, I can get tons of pictures of bucks with their noses in the scrape, and it doesn't alarm them at all.

"In that case, I can end up getting a lot more photos of the same buck than if I were using a flash camera, where he would probably be gone after one or two flashes. Bucks don't seem to pay any attention to the infrared cameras as long as they're positioned up high. I think it's because they don't usually look up at the camera.

> Basically, my goal is to get good, clean pictures of our deer, and I want to be able to see every point clearly and distinctly.

"I like to use infrared cameras on some of my farms that are farther away from where we live. For example, I don't get down to our farm in Kansas as often as I'd like to check the photos. So when I set up my cameras down there, I want to make sure I get more than just two pictures of any individual buck. I want that buck to come back to the spot time after time so that I'll get numerous pictures of him.

"In that case, I'll set up my infrared cameras really high. Sometimes, I'll even use a ladder to put them up as high as 10 or 15 feet off the ground and face them down on a scrape or mineral station. The bucks usually have their heads down in the scrape so they don't even notice the infrared pop, because they seldom look up at the camera.

"Another advantage of having your cameras up high is to get pictures of trespassers and poachers. Trespassers and shed thieves don't usually look up in the trees for cameras, and we have gotten good pictures of several trespassers, as mentioned. So even though I use a combination of both types of camera, most of the cameras we use are flash cameras so we can get good, clear pictures of our deer.

Keeping Track of all Those Photos

"As you might imagine, I have thousands of digital trail-camera photos going back many years. Currently, I have five years of Cuddeback pictures on my desktop at home dating back to 2007. Many times when I go to check the cards in cameras on certain farms, I'll have my laptop with me in the truck so I can download the photos immediately to see what I have. Or I'll take the cards home with me after swapping them out and putting new cards in the cameras, and I'll put the new pictures on my desktop.

"Later when I have time, I'll go through the entire file and delete all of the doe pictures and any other pictures that are of no use. I keep a separate folder for each farm, and I dump all of my new photos into that folder with the date and field where the photos were taken. I back up all of my photos on discs in case my computer crashes.

"I know there are software programs that you can buy to organize photos. So far, my system has worked well for me, but one of these days, I might change to a more sophisticated system."

BUCKS TO DROOL ABOUT AND LESSONS LEARNED

The Backyard Buck

"The same year that Tiffany and I moved to our farm in Iowa (2003), we started getting a lot of pictures of a big deer that scored around 170 inches," Lee said. "I estimated him to be 4½ years old at the time. Until then, that farm had experienced a lot of hunting pressure. Although we had a good number of young 2½- and 3½-year-old bucks, we didn't see many that were older. So seeing that this deer was definitely the best deer we had on the farm that first year, I told my partner John Beneke, who lives in Minnesota, that I had a great deer picked out for him. John came down and hunted the deer, but we never saw him during hunting season that year.

Lee and Tiffany believed the Backyard Buck would have scored about 240 inches during his best year. Here, Tiffany shows off one of the buck's massive sheds.

"The next year, the deer was back, and he had really grown. By this time, he had a 200- to 210-inch nontypical rack. Ironically, because this was the farm where we lived, the only time we ever got pictures of him was in our back yard. I normally put out a feeder in our back yard in the winter after deer season closes so Tiffany and I can watch deer from the house. We never got any pictures of him in any food plots back in the interior of the farm or anywhere else — only in the yard.

"I always loved that deer because we found his sheds, and we saw him so many times right from the house. Several times in December, while hunting season was still in, we had guests over to cook out, and there he was — standing over at the feeder 50 yards away. 'Man, you need to shoot that deer,' people would say, but I wasn't about to shoot a deer in my back yard. He was more like a pet, and the back yard was off limits.

"Like other deer we had known about, he obviously wasn't living on our property during hunting season. But he would always be back in winter, and I couldn't wait to find his sheds every year. The third year we were there, he had grown a nontypical rack that would easily score 240 inches. Even now, after 10 years of living in Iowa, he's still the best deer we've ever seen on any of our farms.

"He was seen only one time during hunting season. Adam Beneke, John's son, was hunting in one of our northern food plots back in the timber, and the big 240 came in with a doe. He never got any closer than 40 yards, but Adam did not feel proficient enough at that range to attempt a shot with a bow. I commend him for that. With a buck of that size, most people would have started flinging arrows.

"The next day, Adam went back out and saw him again in the same spot. But again, the deer never came closer than 40 yards, and Adam refused to try a shot. We did move his stand that afternoon, and Adam hunted there the third day but never saw the buck again. That was the only time any of our hunters ever saw him during hunting season. I found his sheds that year, and they were unbelievable. They had two rows of double tines and a number of sticker points. He was a true monster.

"By the next year, he was at least 8½ years old, and his rack started going downhill. As always, we got some pictures of him again behind the house. Later, during shotgun season, some hunters across the street were doing a deer drive. One of their relatives from Illinois pushed the deer out of a small fence row and shot several times at him. The buck was actually headed back toward our house when the Illinois man made a hail Mary shot with his last slug and hit him in the back of the head at 150 yards, killing him instantly.

"A couple of years later, they brought him to the Iowa Deer Classic and had him officially scored at 227 inches nontypical. The year before — his best year — he had sported a 6-by-6 rack with a lot of inside points and stickers. The year he was killed, his right side was a main frame 4-point, and he had lost some of his stickers, but he still scored 227 inches. Because they shot him across the street, he was probably living there most of the year, and then he would come over to our farm in late season because of the food we had.

> When we first moved to Iowa, I didn't know nearly as much about hunting mature bucks as I know now, and we shot a lot of 3½-year-old bucks.

"I think the story of the Backyard Buck is a prime example of how hunting pressure can move a big deer like that out of one area and into another area that becomes a safe haven. When we first moved to Iowa, I didn't know nearly as much about hunting mature bucks as I know now, and we shot a lot of 3½-year-old bucks. Having just moved from the city where houses are only a few feet apart, I was in heaven living on a wide-open farm, and I was out every day checking cameras, working on food plots, looking for sheds and driving around the property. Because it was the only farm we had, it was the only place we hunted that first season, and there's no doubt in my mind that we overdid it. We were out there every day doing something.

"The spot across the street where the deer was killed was a huge CRP field with a small stand of timber, and the only time anybody ever went in there was a few days a year during shotgun season. So 99 percent of the time, there was no pressure in there whatsoever. I'm sure that deer had been living on our farm to begin with, but the minute we started putting pressure on him, he simply moved across the street where it was safer.

"Like several other older bucks we had known that grew superior racks, we saw from trail-camera photos that the Backyard Buck had gotten very non-aggressive and reclusive. The younger 3½-year-olds intimidated him and could have had something to do with his leaving the farm as well.

By 2009, Barnacle Bill had grown about 40 inches of sticker points around his bases. Lee figured the deer would probably score about 190.

"And just like with Gnarles Barkley, which came on the scene a couple of years later, you're not going to call or rattle in bucks like that. If you try to grunt them in, chances are they'll go the other way. So you have to try to entice them to stay on your farm through food.

"During that same period, we had another deer in there that we called Junior. He was smaller than the Backyard Buck, but he had a nice 6-by-6 rack with several stickers. We saw him several times behind the house as a 3½-year-old and 4½-year-old, but then my neighbor to the north found his sheds on his property. That deer had no doubt left our property because of the pressure we were putting on it.

Those deer taught me a big lesson. That's the fun part about whitetail hunting. You keep learning new things about deer every day. I'm sure that I'm probably doing some things wrong right now that I won't be doing a few years because I keep learning new lessons every season.

The Sad Saga of Barnacle Bill

"In 2008, the year before I shot Gnarles Barkley (see Chapter 5 for full story), one of the biggest bucks we'd ever seen in our area was living on one of our farms. We named him Barnacle Bill because of his unusual rack. I had found his sheds the year before in 2007. He had been a big 10 that year, and he probably would have scored in the mid-170s. At that time, he had a couple of little stickers on each of his bases.

"The next summer, I watched him late in the afternoon almost every day. He would always come out in one area on the pipeline in broad daylight, and he was so at home and so secure because he was well hidden down in a little hollow. By that time, he had grown something like 40 inches of stickers around his bases, and we decided to name him Barnacle Bill. I figured he would probably score around 190 inches.

"I got all kinds of trail camera pictures of him. I just knew I was going to kill him. It was going to be so easy because I had him so figured out.

"I should have gone in there to put up some stands that summer to hunt various winds, but I didn't. I got so busy doing other things that I kept putting it off. I kept telling myself, 'I'll

Lee had numerous photos of Barnacle Bill and had the buck's movements figured out. In fact, he thought killing the deer would be a piece of cake.

do it later.' Pretty soon, September came along, and as usual, we were off hunting in other places for the entire month. Tiffany's brother Jason was checking cameras for me while we were gone. Every day, we had pictures of him taken at 5:30 or 6 p.m. in broad daylight. I just knew that as soon as I got home, he would be mine. Killing him would be a piece of cake.

"We got home Oct. 6 that year. Just like I would be with Gnarles a year later, I was very excited about hunting Barnacle Bill. In fact, I was so excited that I tried to push it. Because I didn't have any stands set up, I figured I'd run out there that afternoon and pop one up. I didn't get out there until about 5 p.m., and I never should have gone that late in the day. Big mistake.

"What I should have done was to wait until the next day, when I had plenty time to get out there early and set up a stand around noon. That way, I could sit all afternoon without being in a hurry and without disturbing anything. But I just got a little carried away because I was so excited, and I knew this buck's habits so well. I decided to put up the stand in a tree I had previously picked out, but the tree didn't cooperate very well. I made a lot of noise, but I finally got it up. Second big mistake.

"Just before dark, one of the bucks that Barnacle Bill was always with came out, but I never saw any sign of Barnacle Bill. According to our cameras, this was probably the first night in several weeks that he hadn't come out.

"No big deal. I figured I just come back and hunt him the next afternoon. So I did. And I hunted him for the rest of that season and never saw him again. We never got another picture of him, and we never saw any sign of him. He had simply vanished. By the end of the season I was thinking, 'What in the world could have happened to him?'

"Late in December, I bumped into my neighbor across the road. 'Guess what?' he told me excitedly. 'I shot a big, old deer late the afternoon of Oct. 6 with my longbow. He scored 206 nontypical points. I had never seen him before, but he came running across the road, and I got him.'

"As you might imagine, I was glad for my neighbor, but I was sick at heart. Barnacle Bill had apparently been right there as usual when I went in to put up my stand. I obviously made too much noise and ran him off. He had apparently never been on my neighbor's property before, and I simply pushed him out of the area. That's an easy thing to do with big mature bucks. As I've said so many times, they don't often give you a second chance.

"I was so mad at myself for being so stupid. I had been so anxious to kill him that I made several big mistakes that day. If I had just waited and done things right, I might have easily gotten a chance at him a day or two later.

"The circumstances were very similar a year later when I was hunting Gnarles at a different farm. Fortunately, I had learned my lesson. Instead of pushing it like I had done with Barnacle Bill, the day we got home from our travels in early October that year, Tiffany and I quietly walked out to the end of trail just to observe the field, and there was Gnarles feeding on clover. I was so thrilled he was there.

"You have to be patient. You have to do things right. So many times when you are hunting a certain stand for a big deer, the wind might not be right, but you're tempted to sneak in there anyway. If you do, you might end up doing the same thing I did with Barnacle Bill. How many big deer are spared each year because hunters get impatient? Bide your time. Pick the right time, the right wind and the right spot. If you rush it like I did, you might never see that buck again.

"I learned a lesson the hard way, and it is a lesson I'll never forget. I had that deer so dead to rights that I had a spot already picked out on my wall for him. I thought he would score around 190 inches, but he ended up having a lot more stickers around his bases than I thought he did.

> Pick the right time, the right wind and the right spot. If you rush it like I did, you might never see that buck again.

Decoys Really Work

"During the late '90s, a year or two before Tiffany decided to start bow-hunting for deer in her own right, she frequently accompanied me on hunts to Kansas and Iowa and several other states. Sometimes, we would use her flight passes to get free airline tickets, and we'd fly all over the place looking for good spots to hunt. We'd always put up two stands and sit in a tree together while I hunted, and we always enjoyed each other's company immensely.

"I had heard great things about Illinois as a big-buck state, and someone showed me some pictures of a giant deer that was taken near a state park in Bloomington. So I decided to go there during the rut and see if I could find a place to hunt near that park. My plan was to knock on doors and ask local farmers if I could hunt on their land.

"As luck would have it, the first farmer I went to said, 'Yes, you can hunt here.' He said he hunted some himself, but he was more than happy to let me bow-hunt his property. The farmer's next-door neighbor was notorious for not allowing any hunting

on his farm, and it just so happened that the neighbor's land was right next to the park, where no hunting was allowed.

"So just like the park area, the neigbor's land was a sanctuary for the local deer. From a distance, I immediately started seeing lots bucks on his property, but they seldom came over the line to the farmer's property where I was hunting because of the moderate hunting pressure.

"I put up a stand in some woods near the neighbor's property line. For several mornings and afternoons in a row, I saw a very nice 6-by-6 buck come out in a certain field some distance away. Even when I wasn't hunting that particular stand, I could still see this big buck with my binoculars from other locations on the farmer's property. It was during the rut in November, and every time I saw that buck, he was out in the field chasing does. He was super aggressive, and every time another smaller buck came out in that field, he would lay back his ears and run the other deer out of the field.

"I had brought a decoy with me, but up until that point, I had never actually used one while actually hunting. Most of my hunting experience had been in Minnesota, where we saw very few bucks, and techniques like rattling and decoying never worked because there were so few deer. So never having had any experience with a decoy, I decided to give it a shot. I had brought some sheds with me that scored around 130 inches, and I drilled some holes in them, put some dowels in and attached them to the decoy. With those real antlers on his head, the decoy looked pretty big.

> That decoy worked like a charm. The buck's ears were pinned back, and his hair was bristled out.

"My plan was to put it out on our side of the ditch to see if I could get that buck's attention. The next morning, I went out and set up the decoy in the dark. Tiffany and I got in the same tree where we'd been watching the big 6-by-6 for the past few days. As usual, he came out and started chasing does around in the field. I tried to make some loud grunts to get his attention, but I don't think he could hear me because of the distance.

"Finally, he chased a doe a little closer to our position, and I grunted again. I don't know if he heard me or if he saw the decoy, but he looked over, and here he came. That decoy worked like a charm. His ears were pinned back, and his hair was all bristled out, and he came right to that decoy. I shot him at 20 yards, and he ran about 50 yards and fell over.

"He probably scored in the 140s. If I had to guess, I'd say he was a 3½-year-old, but he was a super buck for me at the time. Up until then, I'd probably taken only three or four racked bucks, so using that decoy successfully was a great learning experience.

The Big Brow-Tine Buck: Rattling Too Often

"Several years ago, I followed a nice young 8-pointer on one of our farms as a 2½-year-old and then as a 3½. He had extra-long brow tines, and we started calling him the Big Brow-Tine Buck.

"He was a super aggressive deer, and I rattled him in numerous times. In fact, sometimes I would rattle him in, and he would eventually wander off. Then, 15 minutes later, I would hit the horns together, and he would come charging in again. It's always a lot of fun to rattle in a deer like that.

"But guess what? When he reached the age of 4½, he no longer responded to my rattling. By now he was even more aggressive, and he was always running off other deer. And thanks to me and what I had done so many times, he was also educated. I knew we needed to get him out of the herd, and I tried and tried to trip him up during the entire archery season one year, but that deer had gotten way too smart.

"Fortunately, I was able to shoot him with a muzzleloader during the late season. I made a 100-yard shot on him in a bean field. If it hadn't been over late-season food, I probably never would have gotten him. When a deer like that reaches maturity and gets educated, your chances of killing him go down considerably.

"The Big Brow-Tine Buck taught me a big lesson. Now Tiffany and I seldom go out and do any blind rattling or even blind grunting. I prefer to have a buck in sight before I do any type of calling. That way, you can start with a few low grunts or you might simply tickle the antlers together, and then watch to see how the deer responds.

The Big Brow Tine Buck provided a hard lesson: Don't rattle too often, even to 2½- or 3½-year-old deer.

"If he keeps on going, you might want to get a little more aggressive. If he doesn't respond to tickling the antlers or a couple of low grunts, you might want to try a snort-wheeze. The snort-wheeze has worked like a charm for Tiffany and me as a last resort on numerous occasions.

"So be careful when you are calling, especially with blind rattling. You never know what's out there, and young curious bucks itching for a fight might respond to your blind rattling again and again, just like the Big Brow Tine Buck did with me. Big deer learn quickly and they don't forget. When they get wise to you, it's a different ball game.

Thanksgiving Day 2001, Kansas:
The Day We Almost Slept In

"It's great to hunt every day of the season like Tiffany and I do. But if you get up at 4 a.m. every morning and go to bed late at night, it can certainly be exhausting after many days of little sleep. We got in the habit of hunting every day during the season more than 10 years ago when we still lived in Minnesota. I would take off from work a month or five weeks, and Tiffany and I would go down to Kansas and hunt every day until we filled our tag. Back then, our hunting time was so precious, we had to do it. But it took its toll nonetheless.

"In fact, during the 2001 season, we were staying in a motel in northern Kansas during Thanksgiving week with several other out-of-state hunters. Naturally, after a few days of being there, we would all come in after a long day of hunting and do a little socializing. Like us, most of the people staying at the motel were all die-hard hunters. Instead of being home with their families on Thanksgiving Day, they were hunting in Kansas. On Wednesday evening, we talked to several of the others about getting a turkey, cooking it on Thanksgiving Day and sharing a Thanksgiving dinner.

"The next morning, the alarm went off at 4 a.m. Tiffany and I were so tired from hunting every day for the past couple of weeks that we looked at each and said, 'Let's just go back to bed. We can get up later and cook the turkey, and we can go out late in the afternoon for the evening hunt. So that's what we decided to do.

"We shut the alarm off and went back to bed. Less than 10 minutes later, I sat straight up and said, 'No, we can't do it. I've got to be back at work in a few days, and we can't afford to take a morning off. We've got to be out there this morning.' So we put on our hunting clothes and left for the woods.

"In those days, Tiffany and I took turns filming each other. I would usually hunt in the mornings when it was a lot colder, and Tiffany would hunt the afternoons after it had warmed up a bit. We hadn't been seeing much for the past few days, and when we got to our stand that morning, it was just cracking daylight. I said, 'I think I'll grab the antlers and give them a crack or two.'

"Immediately after hitting the antlers together, I heard the leaves rustling off in the distance, and I knew a deer was coming. I quickly hung up the antlers and grabbed my bow. A few seconds later, a nice buck came running in with his ears back and stopped near a scrape under a cedar tree that was about 35 yards away. Tiffany got right on him with the camera. He started walking stiff-legged toward the scrape. I stopped him and shot him at about 35 yards.

"He went tearing off across an open ditch, and we saw him go down on the opposite hillside. We knew he was a good deer, and I told Tiffany that I thought he might score 150 or maybe even 160 inches. But when we got up to him, I said, 'Oh my gosh. He's a lot bigger than a 150 or a 160.' He was huge.

"My good friend Lee Murphy from Minnesota was hunting on a different piece of property with his son Lonny, and I called him and told him about my buck. They came right over, and when they saw the buck they said, 'He's bigger than a 170.'

"After we filmed our recovery and got all of the video footage we needed, we went back to the hotel and put a tape to the rack. He scored 196 inches. He was basically a huge 10-pointer with about 15 inches in sticker points around his bases. To this day, he's still the highest scoring deer I've ever taken anywhere.

"Tiffany and I will never forget what almost happened on that unforgettable morning. It would have been so easy for us to go back to bed. We were exhausted. Today, it seems as though we're even busier than we were back then. We often find ourselves totally exhausted from hunting and working around the farm. We still get up at 4 a.m. every morning during hunting season, but we often have guests hunting with us, and we sometimes don't get to bed until 2 a.m. Then we have to get up the next morning and do it all over again.

"Whenever we get exhausted, it would be so tempting to say, 'Let's just sleep in this one time.' But we always think back to that unbelievable Thanksgiving morning in Kansas, the day we almost didn't go hunting. 'Remember Kansas,' we say. 'We can't afford to sleep in no matter how tired we are. We have to get up and go.'

"Interestingly, two days before I killed that buck, I was in a food plot looking for a spot to put up a stand. While I was looking around on a trail just inside the tree line, I found a huge shed antler with five normal points and several stickers on the bases. So I put up my stand right there, and two days later, I shot the buck that had dropped that shed. Later, as we were leaving, I went in to pull out my stand. When I got up in it and looked out, I saw the point of another antler sticking up. It was the other side to the buck I had just shot. Now I had both sheds from him. How strange is that?"

> Whenever we get exhausted, it would be so tempting to say, "Let's just sleep in this one time."

ON THE ROAD AGAIN

A Memorable Honeymoon and Life-Changing Experience

Whitetail hunting might be an obsession to many people, but how many couples do you know who would go deer hunting on their honeymoon? Probably not too many. However, Lee and Tiffany Lakosky are in a league of their own, and nothing is beyond the realm of possibility. To them, going on a hunting adventure for their honeymoon was the perfect way to celebrate their marriage.

"Tiffany and I got married Aug. 23, 2003," Lee said. "We really didn't have any money for a honeymoon, so when David Blanton of Realtree called and asked us to go on a whitetail hunt with him to the 7J Ranch in Wyoming in early September, we were thrilled beyond belief. We had gotten to know David through the *Monster*

Bucks 10 video he had featured us in that year, and we jumped at the chance to go hunting with him. David was an icon in the hunting industry, and to be asked to go on a hunt with him was the chance of a lifetime.

"Tiffany was just as excited about going on the hunt as I was. And I have to say, when a man picks a wife who wants to go deer hunting on her honeymoon, he knows that he's made the right decision.

"I remember sitting in our room the first evening we were at the ranch and thinking, 'This is unbelievable. David Blanton is actually in the room next to us.' I was in awe of him. He had been one of my hunting idols for a long time, and Tiffany and I had the deepest respect for everyone at Realtree.

"Although we had a great time, nobody shot a deer on that hunt. We saw a lot of good deer, but we were never able to get close to any of them.

However, that trip turned out to be a real turning point in our career. I was not happy working at the refinery any more because deer hunting had taken over my life, and the company was trying to curtail some of my fall hunting trips. That just about killed me. So two weeks after we returned home from that Wyoming hunt, I quit my job, and we moved to Iowa.

"Just being around David and knowing that the Realtree crew wanted us to film hunts for their videos gave me the encouragement I needed to make the decision to try and get into the hunting industry. I knew in my heart that this what I truly wanted to do, and hunting with a real professional like David gave me the courage I needed to make the big plunge. I'd been standing on the high dive, and David gave me the nudge I needed to step off that diving board.

"Tiffany and I didn't have any money, and we didn't know how we were going to do it. In fact, I would have been happy shining David Blanton's shoes. That's how bad I wanted to make a living doing what I loved so much. But we did have a lot of determination and faith, and that helped get us on the road to a career that has been unbelievable in so many ways.

Touring in the Legendary Lakosky Bus

"From the time Tiffany and I first met, we always did a lot of traveling together. As time went one, we started hunting every day during hunting season, from early September to mid-January. After that, we started doing a lot of appearances during the off-season at deer shows and sporting goods stores such as Cabela's and Bass Pro.

"As Tiffany mentioned in Chapter 2, traveling by air became a real dilemma for us. If we were hunting, we always had at least two cameramen going with us plus a lot of extra bags that we got charged for. Our travel budget got very expensive. If we were doing weekend appearances, just trying to get to most destinations took a full day to get there and a full day to return home. Since all of that down time was a complete waste of time, I knew there had to be a better way.

"I've always been a huge country music fan, and eight or nine years ago, Tiffany and I started going to some weekend concerts and hanging out with several country singers. They all had buses that they toured in, and those buses became their homes away from home. We sometimes hooked up with them on the road, and we saw how nice it was for those country singers to travel to their weekend performances on their custom buses. They could take the entire band and pull a trailer behind with all of their instruments. I thought, 'Man that would really be nice if Tiffany and I could do the same thing.'

"One of my sisters worked at an RV place, and in 2005, Tiffany and I rented an RV for the entire month of September to use while we were away from home hunting. We packed up all our gear and our two cameramen and took off. It worked out so

Lee and Tiffany's bus lets them avoid the hassle and cost of air travel while providing the comforts of home.

well. For the first time ever, we could travel at our own pace and not have to work around the airline's schedule. We saved time and money.

"The next year, we rented an even larger RV. That worked out well, too, but we knew that traveling by bus was much more comfortable. The springs on a bus are a lot different, and you just glide along and hardly know you're moving. RVs have a much bumpier ride.

"About that time, we had gotten to know Kylie Irvin, who owns Diamond Coach Co. in Nashville. Her company outfits buses for a lot of the country singers. In 2007, we worked out a deal with her to lease a bus for the entire hunting season. That worked so well, and ended up saving us a lot of time as well as money in air travel.

"The next year, our good friend Gary LeVox, of Rascal Flatts fame — who hunts with us in Iowa every year — was getting a new bus, and he asked Kylie to give us a special deal on his old bus. She did, and we were able to lease Gary's old bus at a very reasonable price. We put the logos of most of our sponsors on the sides of the bus, and they helped us out with the lease.

"Having that bus has made things so much easier for us. Now, instead of losing several days in travel time, Tiffany and I can go on a hunt or make an appearance somewhere and then go to bed. The bus drives all night, and by the time we wake up the next morning, we're home. We can also edit video on the bus while we are traveling, work on computers, answer e-mails and do all sorts of things that we couldn't do previously. It's been a win-win situation for us all the way around.

"Some people have said that we're just trying to big shots by traveling around in a bus. Nothing could be farther from the truth. Using that bus has nothing to do with status. Getting it was purely a business decision. Tiffany and I probably do more appearances each year than anyone else in the hunting industry. In Winter 2011 after hunting season, we were on the road for 14 weeks in a row making appearances. Having that bus made it all possible.

"During the past few years, it has saved us thousands of dollars in expenses and given us back many days that would have been wasted in airports, not to mention the comfort of traveling in it on long, exhausting road trips. In all, leasing that bus has been one of the best things we've ever done, and we love it."

Linda's Life-Changing Bear Hunt in Alberta

Tiffany's mom, Linda Profant, was a city girl and never hunted. She and Tiffany's dad, Gary, had done a lot of fishing at their cabin in northern Minnesota while Tiffany was growing up, but hunting was as foreign to her as traveling to the moon.

After Lee and Tiffany were married, they frequently sent Linda pictures of themselves posed with some of the trophy deer they had taken in Iowa and Kansas. This was a big point of contention with Linda. She would always cut out the dead deer in the pictures and keep only the portion that showed Lee and Tiffany.

Soon after Lee and Tiffany moved to Iowa, Linda started coming down from Minneapolis to visit regularly. During hunting season, when Lee and Tiffany were hosting more guests, she started helping with the cooking and other chores. Her cooking quickly became legendary with the guests. It wasn't long before she packed up and moved to Iowa permanently. Lee and Tiffany were thrilled when she did.

"She knew absolutely nothing about hunting," Lee said. "But after she started coming down to visit, she could see how much fun we were having with all of our guests. We would sit around at night and play guitars and view video footage, and she quickly realized that hunting was not entirely about shooting animals. It was about hanging out with family and friends, and the camaraderie and good times that went with it.

"After a couple of years of seeing how much fun we were having, she came up to us one day out of the clear blue and said, 'I'd like to shoot a turkey and a bear.'

Linda Profant, Tiffany's mom, knew little about hunting when she moved to Iowa. After a while, however, she decided to go on a bear hunt.

"Tiffany and I were floored. But it just so happened that we were planning to go on a bear hunt in Alberta that year (2008), and we invited her to come along. We got her a muzzleloader, and she started practicing with it using 100 grains of powder. She was an unusually good shot from the start. She never flinched, and she always hit whatever she was aiming at. We would fill up water bottles, and she hit them every time at 100 yards.

"When we got to Canada, we put out a camera in a small clearing planted in clover that had been a former test site for oil and gas drilling. Almost immediately, we got some pictures of a very good bear. Everyone wanted to be involved in Linda's hunt. It was clear from the start that it was going to be a family affair. We decided to build a small brush blind on the ground so that we could all get in it and let Linda try to shoot one from the ground. Ordinarily, most bear hunting in Alberta is done from an elevated tree blind or tree stand.

> Shooting that bear was the most exciting thing I've ever done in my entire life.

"On the day of the hunt, Linda, Tiffany, our guide Tom Wayne and I got in the blind together. Just like clockwork, the bear came out in the field and started pawing around for dandelions and clover. Linda was so calm. She never got nervous. She was much like Tiffany had been on the day she shot her first buck. I told Linda to get the cross-hairs on the bear, wait for a perfect shot and squeeze the trigger when everything felt right.

"Linda made a perfect shot, and the bear went about 50 yards and dropped. Now she was excited. She was jumping up and down much like Tiffany had done on her first buck, and she couldn't wait to take pictures, call all her friends and tell everyone that she had killed a bear. 'Shooting that bear was the most exciting thing I've ever done in my entire life,' she later said. And she was serious. It affected her that much.

"Linda's been hooked on hunting ever since. Since that bear hunt, she's taken a couple of turkeys with her bow, and lately she's been doing a lot of practicing in anticipation of shooting a deer. One of these days in the near future, I'm sure it will happen.

Alberta Velvet Buck

"Tiffany and I have been hunting early season in Alberta for several years. Back in September 2007, we were joined by Don and Kandi Kisky. Our guide, Larry Jolliffe, of Northern Wilderness Outfitters, had been watching some of the alfalfa fields in late summer. He had seen a couple of big bucks coming out and feeding at one side of a large field.

"So soon after we arrived, Larry, Tiffany and I went out at mid-

day to put up a couple of stands in the area where he'd been seeing those bucks. We hunted there the first afternoon, and we saw a couple of decent bucks come out, but they weren't quite big enough to go after. However, I saw a really big buck come out from the opposite corner of the field about 250 to 300 yards away.

"The next morning about 10 a.m., after we were sure the deer were off the field and back in their bedding areas in the deep timber, we went in and moved a stand over to the spot where I had seen the big one come out. There were visible trails close to the spot where I hung my stand, and I wasn't sure where the buck had come out. He had more or less appeared the evening before. So I got in my stand and waited.

"Late that afternoon, at last light, I saw him coming through a thick, grown-up area that had been clear cut. He was coming down an old logging road, and the brush on either side of him was probably 8 to 10 feet tall. There were no trees in there at all; just a lot of high, nasty brush.

"He finally disappeared from view. I wasn't sure where he was going to reappear near the edge of the field, where he would have to jump a fence. Then, all at once, much like the afternoon before, there he was — out in the field about 60 yards from my

Lee's velvet-covered Alberta buck, shot in September 2007, scored in the high 160s.

261

stand. He started quartering in our general direction, and when he closed the distance to about 40 yards, I was able to make a good shot on him. He was a beautiful 10-pointer that scored in the high 160s.

"That hunt was not unlike so many others we've been on in years past. Like we do in most places during the early season, we made sure the wind was right and put up an observation stand the first afternoon out. Then we watched to see what the deer were doing. When we saw where the big one was coming out of the woods, we adjusted accordingly by putting up a new stand.

> When we see what the bucks are doing and where they are coming out, we adjust our game plan and move in.

"Don Kisky had seen another big buck in another field. A couple of days later, I helped him move his stand closer to the spot where he had seen the big one. That new location was more or less an observation stand to watch from and see what was going on in the area. The first afternoon he hunted it, a 180-inch velvet giant came out, and he shot it instead of the buck he had seen earlier.

"For Tiffany and me, hunting in Alberta is a lot like hunting in Iowa during early bow season. We're usually gone the entire month of September, and even though we watch certain bucks all summer before we leave in late August, we don't really know what our bucks have been doing during September when we return home because we've been gone for a month.

"So to start with at least, we do more observing than we do hunting on the edges of the fields where we had seen certain bucks in August, and we watch to see what they are doing. When we see what the bucks are doing and where they are coming out, we adjust our game plan and move in.

Yukon Moose:
Sometimes You Win, Sometimes You Lose

"We'd been moose hunting several times, but until the 2009 season, I had never shot a moose before. That year, I was lucky enough to go to the Yukon on a moose hunt with Jim Shockey. On the first day out, we saw a giant moose. Most hunters would have put an arrow in that moose immediately. But I didn't want my hunt to end so quickly, so after thinking about it, I passed on him.

"When we got back to the lodge that night, we viewed the footage we had taken, and everyone there said, 'You must be nuts. I can't believe you didn't shoot that moose. You'll never get another chance at an animal like that.'

"They were probably right. Nine times out of 10, if you pass

Lee's 2009 Yukon moose, shot on the final day of his hunt, had a green score of about 240.

up a big whitetail or any other kind of animal, you might not get another chance. But to my way of thinking, you'll never shoot a 170-inch whitetail if you shoot the first 150 you see. It was the same situation with moose, and I had no problem whatsoever passing up that bull. More than anything else, I wanted to enjoy the experience.

"We hunted hard for six days. On the sixth day, we saw a much bigger and higher-scoring bull. I was able to make a great stalk on him as well as a good shot. His gross green score was about 240 inches. I was told that my moose might be the No. 3 all-time moose in the *Pope and Young Record Book*. However, although I believe the animal should always get the recognition it deserves, Tiffany and I have never been into official scores or entering trophies in the record book.

"Some times you win, sometimes you lose. In my case, I had the hunt of a lifetime and ended up shooting a moose that went way beyond my wildest expectations. But if I hadn't filled my tag, I would have enjoyed the hunt nonetheless. Tiffany and I have never taken the attitude that we have to go out and kill something every time we go out. To us, being there and enjoying the experience is the thing that really matters. Yes, being successful is important, but the camaraderie and the anticipation of the hunt are the things that matter to us the most.

A Wolf for the Ages

"In 2007, Tiffany and I went to Alberta to bow-hunt for bears with our good friends at Northern Wilderness Outfitters. I was in a tree waiting for a bear when all of a sudden, I saw a flash of something going through the woods. At first I thought it was

In 2007, Lee became one of the few hunters in North America to take a timber wolf with archery equipment.

a blond bear. A closer look revealed that it was not a bear — it was a light-colored wolf.

"In Alberta, there is no closed season on wolves, and you can shoot them year-round. But they are never easy animals to kill, even with a rifle. They always seem to have a sixth sense when someone is around, and they always seem to be on the move. They always sneak through the woods like a ghost. They seldom just stand there and offer you a shot.

"As soon as I realized I was looking at a wolf, I noted which way it was going. Then I picked a hole in the brush at 42 yards. Just as it reached that opening, I released my arrow. It was a good shot, and I had my first wolf."

Note: Lee is one of only a handful of hunters in North America who has taken a wolf with a bow.

Tiffany's Drop-Tine Buck

"It's very ironic, but I've taken three bucks that score in the mid-170s," Tiffany said. "All three were taken in Iowa. One is the buck I call Unicorn, which I shot with my bow in the late season. We never saw him until he was 4½ years old. He was one of those bucks that came over to our farm in late season because of the food and apparently decided to stay. I got him the next season in late December.

"Another is my big drop-tine buck that I shot while hunting with Kandi Kisky. And the third buck was taken with a muzzleloader late in the season the same year that I shot the drop-tine buck on one of our farms close to home. They're such different deer, but they all score about 174 to 175 inches. Although they're all incredible trophies, one of these days I hope to shoot one that scores in the 180s or 190s.

"In 2003, Lee and I had been hunting in Kansas during the rut in November, but I wasn't having much luck. I left without filling my tag. On the way home, I called my good friend Kandi Kisky to see how she and Don had been making out during the rut. They live about two hours west of us in Iowa, and it happened they both had tagged out on their farm. While we were talking, Kandi said, 'Why don't you stop by and hunt with us for a day or two?'

Tiffany's 2003 Iowa drop-tine buck, shot with friend Kandi Kisky, was a huge-framed 6-by-4.

"The rut was in full swing, and it didn't take much coaxing to accept her invitation. The first afternoon out, things happened rather quickly as soon as we got to our stand. Kandi was filming for me, and we heard a buck grunting. We looked over, and a huge buck was chasing a doe in our direction. He came right by our tree, and I had a fairly easy bow shot at 20 yards.

"What an awesome buck he turned out to be. He was a huge-framed 6-by-4 with three drop-tines — two short and one long — on his left side. I was thrilled beyond words.

Tiffany's Montana Elk: Making It Look Easy

"We were hunting in tree stands in the timber on the edge of a large alfalfa field with Jackie Bushman in 2007 at Fort Musselshell Outfitters. All three of us — Lee, Jackie and me — were spaced out in tree stands on the edge of the alfalfa. This bull came out of the woods bugling his head off, and I smoked

Lee and Tiffany also love elk hunting out West. In 2007, Tiffany shot a huge bull on the edge of an alfalfa field.

him at 51 yards. Everyone else could see me when I made my shot. It was so neat to watch that bull. It was a great hunt.

Tiffany's Caribou

"It was the last minute of the last day of hunting in Quebec. Lee and I were hunting caribou in 2004 with our good friends David Blanton and John Tate at Mirage Outfitters. We had hunted hard for several days, but a snowstorm had shut things down, and the caribou were not moving.

"Suddenly we saw them way off in the distance. They were coming our way, so we decided to sit and wait for them. They came up and started passing by us one by one. I took my time, and finally a really good bull appeared. I ranged him at 51 yards and made a perfect shot. What an exciting hunt."

Caribou? Lee and Tiffany have those covered, too.

AFTERWORD

By Lee Lakosky

I've mentioned this before, but one of the comments we hear from people again and again is, "If I could hunt the Lakosky farm, I'd be killing big deer too." I agree. Tiffany and I realize how fortunate we are to do the things we do and hunt the quality of deer we get to hunt. But it wasn't always that way.

As mentioned in Chapter 1, I didn't shoot my first deer until I was 16. I'd been hunting with my dad since I was 9 years old, and during that time, I probably didn't see a dozen deer. Hunting in northern Minnesota was the toughest of the tough. We were lucky to just see a deer in those days. But I refused to give up, and I became a better hunter through trial, error and experience.

Ten years ago, I didn't own any good property to hunt on. Most of the land I hunted on was public land. But I had a passion for deer hunting, and that's all I ever wanted to do. If you do what you love to do, anything can happen. I never expected to have a TV show or have the property that we have now, but it just goes to show that dreams can come true.

If you just keep after it, sooner or later things start to happen. In 2003, Tiffany and I were able to buy one small piece of land. We would have been perfectly happy with that one small farm. But one thing led to another, and pretty soon we were able to acquire several other tracts.

Shooting a big buck is not as easy as it might appear. There have been plenty of seasons where Tiffany and I each went many long weeks without shooting a deer. And we hunt every day of the season. A few years ago, I hunted 58 days straight, and Tiffany hunted something like 47 days in a row for two years running before she tagged a deer. That's more time than most people hunt during a several-year period.

So it's not always as easy as it looks. By the same token, we realize how very lucky we are. Not many people get to do what we get to do. But we started out at rock bottom like everyone else. And talk about your average guy. That was me 10 or 12

years ago. Even back then, though, we were shooting good deer on public land in Kansas and Iowa because we had a passion for what we were doing. We started out shooting 120-inch deer like everyone else. Then we began to move up the ladder to 130s and 140s, and pretty soon we were targeting older, mature deer because to our way of thinking, 5½-year-old deer were the ultimate bow-hunting challenge.

If deer hunting is your passion and you think about whitetails 24-7, you'll figure out a way to be successful at it just like we did. That's how Olympians are made, and that's how boxers, bikers or UFC fighters become champions. In my case, I wasn't born with a silver deer spoon in my mouth. I always wanted to shoot a Pope and Young buck, but I failed many times before it finally happened.

The bucks I hunted outsmarted me time after time, and I was 22 years old before I shot my first buck with a bow — a little forkie at that. Now, whenever I'm at a deer show somewhere, little 8- and 9-year-old children are always coming up to me and showing me pictures of the giant bucks they've taken. And I always tell them, 'Man, you're a way better hunter than I was at your age. I was 22 before I shot my first buck.'

Nothing comes easy in this world. If you want something badly enough in this life, though, you can make it happen. If your dream is to shoot a big whitetail, never give up. Do everything within your power to make that dream come true, and one of these days, when you're least expecting it, it'll happen.

DEER &
DEER HUNTING
MAGAZINE
PRESENTS
ShopDeerHunting.COM
Get the best insight on:
• Whitetail Rut Predictions
• Deer Behavior
• Hunting Strategies
• Tracking & Trailing
• Food Plots
• Processing & Recipes
Save BIG on everyday deals!
New products being added daily! Watch our weekly newsletters for updates.
PLUS! ... Become a Deer & Deer Hunting Insider and save an Extra 10% on all purchases!
www.shopdeerhunting.com